LETTS CREATIVE NEEDLECRAFTS

EMBROIDERING
TABLE LINEN

· JAN · EATON ·

LETTS CREATIVE NEEDLECRAFTS

EMBROIDERING TABLE LINEN

JAN EATON

CHARLES LETTS · *Letts* · FOUNDED 1796

First published 1990
by Charles Letts & Company Ltd
Diary House, Borough Road
London SE1 1DW

Designed and produced by Rosemary Wilkinson
30 Blackroot Road, Sutton Coldfield, B74 2QP

Illustrator: Elsa Godfrey
Designer: Patrick Knowles
Photographer: Pablo Keller

© Charles Letts & Company Ltd 1990

CIP catalogue record for this book is available from the British Library

ISBN 1 85238 108 6

Typeset by Fakenham Photosetting Ltd, Fakenham, Norfolk

Printed in Belgium

CONTENTS

A selection of early twentieth century table linen

DESIGN: PAST AND PRESENT

Styles in table linen have mirrored changing tastes in interior
decoration, from formal to informal and from plain to
richly embroidered.

Table linen, also known as napery, originally
consisted of those fabric accessories which
were required to dress a dining table for formal
eating. The items consisted of a large cloth to
cover the table completely, matching napkins
in several sizes, doilies, fingerbowl mats and
glass mats. Today, the term covers both formal
and informal table settings, and includes cloths
for tea and breakfast trays and covers for
occasional tables.

Before the nineteenth century, table linen
was made from damask or woven linen fabric,
and tablecloths were usually plain, relying for
effect on the decorative pattern woven into the
fabric. The tablecloths were used with a vast
number of napkins of different shapes and
sizes. During the first part of the nineteenth
century, white, hand embroidered table linen
began to become fashionable and, although
many middle-class women practised
embroidery as a leisure time activity, vast

quantities of this kind of table linen were
commercially embroidered by a large army of
poorly-paid and exploited women outworkers.

The embroidery was stitched on woven
linen fabric even though this was a high cost
material due to the slow, labour-intensive
process of manufacture. Linen, which is made
from flax, has stronger fibres than cotton,
launders well and the fabric has an attractive,
glossy appearance when freshly starched and
pressed. Linen articles were held in such high
regard that old, worn ones were constantly
recycled. Small traycloths and napkins were
cut from worn or damaged tablecloths, and old
napkins had sound portions of their fabric
rescued, embellished with embroidery, edged
with lace or cutwork and turned into doilies
for standing under tureens and serving dishes.

Table linen formed a considerable part of an
unmarried girl's trousseau, 'hope chest' or
'bottom drawer', together with clothing and

other items of household linen. At the turn of the century, the minimum amount of table linen thought to be desirable for a trousseau included four breakfast cloths, four large tablecloths for dinner and four plain cloths for servants' use, two 'best' cloths for formal occasions and twelve napkins for each of these groups.

Whitework, a term which encompasses several styles of white embroidery on white fabric, was used to varying degrees on most articles of table linen, although small cloths and matching napkins for afternoon tea were decorated in a more colourful and elaborate fashion. These were embroidered in a variety of stitches including satin stitch and daisy stitch, often using a riot of brightly-coloured silk threads. Favourite designs were intricate floral patterns, raised monograms and heavy, complex borders.

Many afternoon tea cloths were decorated with areas of cutwork, in which the design is outlined with buttonhole stitch and portions of the background fabric are then cut away. The finest pieces were much prized and often remained unused and carefully stored away in the linen press for several generations, becoming treasured articles which passed down through the family from mother to daughter, thus acquiring the status of family heirlooms.

By the end of the century, due to the steady mechanization of the textile industry, cheap machine embroidered table linen edged with machine-made lace had become widely available. Cotton fabric began to be used for everyday tablecloths and napkins in preference to linen as it was less expensive, but these articles were still referred to as 'linens'.

Hand embroidery remained a popular pursuit for many women throughout the first half of the twentieth century, together with crochet and hand knitting, and enjoyably filled many hours of spare time at home before the advent of television. Many of the attractive tablecloths which survive from the thirties and

The popular crinoline-skirted lady design

forties were in fact purchased in kit form from catalogues and drapers shops. The kits consisted of a linen or cotton cloth with pre-finished edges and a transfer-printed design ready to be stitched using the supplied threads. Designs varied from multi-coloured, naturalistic patterns right through to strong abstract designs with an art deco influence. One design popular throughout the period featured a lady wearing a crinoline-skirted dress and a large picture hat standing on a garden path surrounded by flowers. It was stitched onto tablecloths, mats or traycloths.

Transfers could also be purchased separately and were often given away as gifts with the popular women's magazines of the day, together with suggestions for suitable fabric and thread colours. The design outlines were printed on the transfer paper with a waxy ink, and were transferred to the fabric by pressing with a hot domestic iron. Transfers could, with care, be used more than once.

Less emphasis was put on table linen during the post-war period. Interior design styles changed radically and there was no place for fussy, elaborate table dressing, except on very formal occasions. Furniture became streamlined so styles of table linen had to change. Tablemats in plain bright colours with matching or contrasting napkins were great favourites, contrasting with polished wood tables, stainless steel cutlery and modern china decorated with strong abstract patterns. Polished surfaces were protected from hot serving dishes with heat-resistant mats. For formal occasions, tablecloths were still

preferred, although these too reflected the designs of the period. The restrained Scandinavian styles of embroidery, such as Hardanger work, and geometric designs in cross stitch were much in demand during this period.

By the late sixties, 'contemporary' furniture and large abstract designs began to be replaced by stripped pine and a 'back to nature' approach to home furnishings. Textile designs changed from the brightly-coloured abstracts of the previous years and reflected a growing rediscovery of natural forms. The pine surfaces, often lovingly stripped and waxed by hand, were set with pretty floral printed cloths and napkins, rush or cork mats and hand-thrown stoneware plates and dishes. Inexpensive foreign holidays encouraged more people to travel abroad and many brought back pieces of table linen decorated with peasant embroidery.

Today, due to a strong revival of interest in all things Victorian and Edwardian, the formally dressed table complete with sparkling crystal and silverware is once more popular, providing the perfect design element in an elaborately decorated room. Pieces of antique table linen have recently become eminently collectable, with fine examples commanding very high prices. With more leisure time available and a growing awareness of the pleasures of making things by hand, more and more men and women have begun to enjoy the craft and skills of embroidery, creating beautiful things to use and appreciate in the future.

The designs in this book range from simple projects suitable for the beginner to those for the experienced stitcher. Initially, choose a project which you feel is within your scope, progressing to the more challenging designs when you have gained experience in handling fabrics and thread.

FABRICS

When selecting a fabric for embroidery, choose one which is firmly woven and sufficiently strong to take the weight of the embroidery, avoiding loosely woven fabrics which stretch. Always buy the best quality you can afford so the finished article will wear well, giving you pleasure for many years.

There are two groups of fabric used for embroidery: plain-weave fabrics and even-weave fabrics. Plain-weave is any fabric where the weft yarns weave alternately over and under the warp yarns.

When working with plain-weave, the outline of the design is usually transferred on to the fabric to act as a guide when stitching (as described on page 24). Pure cotton, linen and cotton/synthetic blends are all suitable for making table linen. Plain-weave fabrics with a regular printed or woven pattern, such as polka dots, stripes and checks provide a regular grid for working embroidery stitches like cross stitch and herringbone stitch.

The second group, even-weave fabrics, are a type of plain-weave fabric with a distinctive construction. The warp and weft threads are of identical thickness and the weave is perfectly regular, giving an even number of warp and weft threads in a given area. This number is called the gauge, or the count, of the fabric and is expressed as the number of threads, or blocks of threads, per inch (2.5 cm). The larger the number of threads, the finer the fabric. The regular grid of this type of fabric enables designs to be worked accurately by counting the threads and following a chart. This group also contains fabrics such as Hardanger, Aida and Binca which have threads woven together in pairs or regular blocks. Even-weave fabrics are made from pure cotton or linen or blends of these with synthetics.

THREADS

Embroidery threads are available in a wide range of weights and colours. The following threads have been used for the table linen in this book:

Stranded cotton – a lustrous thread made up of six loosely-twisted strands, which can be separated for fine work.

Perlé cotton – a twisted, shiny 2 ply thread which cannot be divided.

Coton à broder – like perlé cotton, although softer, finer and without the sheen.

Soft embroidery cotton – a thick, twisted thread with a matt finish.

NEEDLES

Unlike plain sewing needles, those for hand embroidery have long eyes to make threading easier. They are numerically graded in size with high numbers denoting the finer needles. The eye of the needle should accommodate the thread easily and the needle should be of the right size to draw through the fabric without pulling it out of shape. Needle sizes are suggested in the instructions for each project, but you may prefer to substitute a different size according to your personal preference. There are three basic types of needle:

Crewel needles – sharp, medium length needles used for fine and medium weight embroidery on plain-weave fabrics.

Chenille needles – similar to crewel needles, but longer and thicker with larger eyes. Use with heavier fabrics and threads.

Tapestry needles – similar in shape to chenille needles but with a blunt end rather than a sharp point. Use for embroidery on even-weave fabrics and for the threading stage of complex embroidery stitches.

HOOPS AND FRAMES

Working with the fabric mounted in an embroidery hoop or frame is more comfortable and will enable you to stitch more evenly, minimizing fabric distortion.

Embroidery hoops – two-part wooden, plastic or metal hoops which take a small area of the fabric and which can be moved across the fabric as the stitching progresses.

Rotating frames – adjustable, accommodating the whole piece of fabric. Useful for working embroidery on items like table mats and napkins, but not suitable for a large piece of work like a tablecloth, for which a hoop would be used. How to use each type is described on page 16.

OTHER EQUIPMENT

There are several other small pieces of equipment which are essential – sharp embroidery scissors, dressmaking scissors, thimble, tape measure, dressmaking pins, ordinary sewing needles and threads. You will also need graph and tracing paper, pencils, ruler and either dressmaker's carbon paper or a transfer pencil.

Good lighting, preferably from an adjustable lamp fitted with a daylight simulation bulb, is important as is a comfortable chair of the right height with good back support.

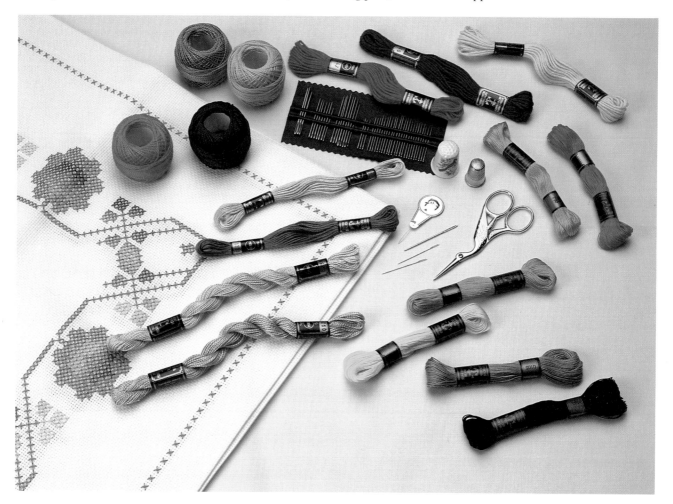

Preparing threads

Use threads in approximately 38 cm (15 in) lengths. A longer thread will tend to tangle in the needle, fray and lose its lustre as it is pulled through the fabric.

If you are using a large amount of a particular colour it saves time if you divide each skein of thread into convenient lengths before you begin to stitch. Cut a strip of stiff card 38 cm (15 in) long, wind the thread round and round its length, then cut across the thread at each end. Make a loose plait from the cut lengths and remove each length as required by pulling one end gently from the plait.

Threading the needle

Thick embroidery threads can be difficult to thread through the needle, but there are three ways to simplify this.

Using a purchased needlethreader – This is a small piece of metal or plastic with a wire loop at one end. Pass the loop through the needle eye, place the end of the thread in the loop and draw the loop and thread through the eye (diagram 1).

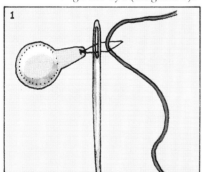

Loop method – Loop the end of the thread round the needle top and grip tightly between finger and thumb. Slide the loop off the needle and insert it still doubled through the needle eye (diagram 2).

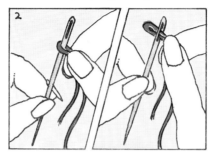

Paper strip method – Cut a strip of paper about 5 cm (2 in) long and narrow enough to pass through the needle eye. Fold the strip in half lengthwise over the end of the thread. Thread the paper through the needle eye, pulling the thread through (diagram 3).

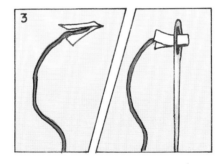

Starting and finishing threads

Do not tie a knot at the end of the thread when you start stitching. This may show through the finished piece of work and will make an unsightly lump on the right side. The knot may also come undone during laundering, causing your stitching to unravel.

Instead, secure the thread in the fabric by making one or two tiny stitches in a space that will be covered by embroidery. Alternatively, leave an end of approximately 5 cm (2 in) which can be darned in later. When working an area which is already partly stitched, secure the new thread on the wrong side by sliding the needle under a group of stitches, anchoring about 2.5 cm (1 in) of thread underneath them. To finish a length of thread, slide the needle under a group of stitches on the wrong side and cut off the loose end.

Using an embroidery hoop

Embroidery hoops are available in various sizes. They consist of two sections, placed one inside the other with the fabric sandwiched in between, which are tightened by a screw at the side of the larger hoop. Bind the smaller hoop, without the screw, with thin cotton tape to help prevent the fabric working loose and sagging as the embroidery proceeds. The tape will also help avoid damage to delicate fabrics.

To mount the fabric, spread the area to be worked right side up over the smaller hoop and press the larger hoop down over the top. Tighten the screw slightly until the larger hoop fits snugly round the smaller hoop. Gently pull the fabric by hand until it is evenly stretched, then tighten the screw fully.

When working on a design which is too large to fit completely inside the hoop, move the hoop along after one portion is completed. Protect the stitches already worked by spreading a piece of tissue paper or muslin over the right side of the embroidery before it is remounted in the hoop. Cut away the paper or muslin carefully to expose the next area to be worked (diagram 4). Loosen the screw and remove the larger hoop whenever you stop work for a long period of time.

Using a rotating frame
This type of frame has the advantage of stretching the fabric very evenly, keeping warp and weft threads at right angles. It consists of top and bottom rollers with strips of webbing attached and two side pieces secured with wing nuts.

Mark the centre of the webbing on both the rollers, also mark the centre of the top and bottom of the fabric. Matching up the marks, stitch the fabric securely to the webbing always beginning at the centre point and working outwards. Use back stitch (page 48) or herringbone stitch (page 57) and a strong thread. Loosen the nuts on the side pieces and slot in the rollers. If the fabric is too long, take up the slack by winding it round one of the rollers. Tighten the nuts firmly (diagram 5).

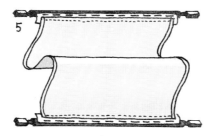

Next, lace the sides of the fabric to the sides of the frame with strong thread, leaving a length free at top and bottom. Tighten the lacing from the centre outwards, working on each side alternately to give an equal tension to the fabric. Secure the thread ends by knotting them round the frame. It is important to get the tension even over the whole surface of the fabric and you may need to make several adjustments (diagram 6).

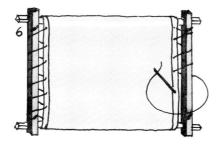

Preparing woven fabrics
During manufacture the fabric weave may become distorted, so that the warp and weft threads are no longer at perfect right angles.

To correct distorted fabric, first straighten the ends either by tearing from one selvage across to the other (firmly-woven fabrics) or by drawing a thread across the fabric, then cutting along the pulled thread (even-weave fabrics). Thoroughly moisten the fabric by spraying with water, fold in half lengthwise matching selvages and raw edges, then tack around the edge. Gently but firmly stretch the fabric on the bias, so that all the corners form right angles and the surface is smooth. Lay the fabric on a flat surface to dry, then remove the tacking and press if necessary.

Quantities
Quantities of fabric and threads have not been given for each project. Instead, there are detailed instructions describing how to measure up and calculate your personal fabric requirements.

You should be able to estimate the amount of thread required by using one complete skein of each colour and measuring how much of the design is then completed. Some of the projects, for example the napkins shown on page 34, use less than one skein of each colour and are the ideal way to use up any oddments of stranded cotton you may have.

CUTWORK TRAYCLOTH

A cutwork floral design embroidered
in shades of yellow, green and orange is repeated
at each end of this delicate traycloth.

Usually worked in white thread on white linen fabric, cutwork is one of the group of traditional embroidery techniques known as whitework. Here, the technique has been brought up to date by the clever use of subtly-coloured embroidery threads to contrast with the cream background.

Make the traycloth larger or smaller by working more or fewer scallops as required between the cutwork motifs. The design can also be adapted to decorate an oval tablecloth. Instructions for cutting an oval cloth are given on page 20. To do this, arrange several motifs round the edge of the oval, spacing them out at regular intervals, and link them together with lengths of the scalloped edging. Alternatively, link the motifs by working one of the scalloped edgings shown on page 80.

REQUIREMENTS

Cream, firmly-woven cotton
   or linen fabric, see next
   page for amount
Coton à broder in the
   following colours: cream,
   soft yellow, light orange,
   dark orange, brown,
   grass green

Crewel needle size 6
Medium embroidery hoop
Sharp embroidery scissors

MEASURING UP

Measure the length and width of the inside of your tray and add at least 5 cm (2 in) all round to allow you to mount the edge of the design comfortably in the embroidery hoop while stitching (diagram 1).

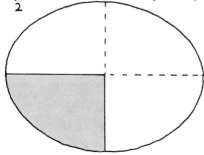

To make an oval tablecloth, first measure the length and width of the table top, then decide how far the cloth will hang down over the edge of the table and add twice this measurement to each of the table top measurements. Finally, add at least 5 cm (2 in) to each measurement, so that you can mount the fabric in the hoop.

Make a paper pattern to fit one quarter of the oval table top exactly

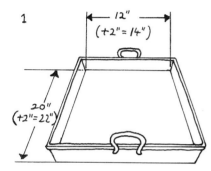

(diagram 2). Join lengths of fabric as required (page 40), then fold in four as for a circular tablecloth (page 40). Pin the paper pattern on to the fabric as shown, then measure the depth of the overhang (and the extra required to mount in the hoop) down from both edges of the pattern. Mark a line on the fabric with a dressmaker's pencil, carefully following the curve of the pattern and keeping the line equidistant from the pattern edge. Cut out along the marked line. Remove the tacking stitches and open out the cloth.

WORKING THE EMBROIDERY

Enlarge or reduce the design (page 21) to the required size and transfer it to the fabric using one of the methods described on page 24. Mount the fabric in the embroidery hoop (page 16).

Using the crewel needle and the appropriate thread colour for each motif as indicated on the diagram, work two lines of running stitch (page 48) following the double outlines of the design. This is necessary to strengthen the edges which will be cut away later. Keep the lines of stitching well inside the double outlines.

Work buttonhole stitch (page 49) in the same colours along the design outlines to cover the running stitches. Use 6 strands of thread throughout. Work the stitches close together, so that both the lines of

running stitch and the ground fabric are completely covered.

Pick out the linear details in stem stitch (page 48), then work groups of three tiny satin stitches (page 56) at the centre of each flower.

MAKING UP

When all the embroidery has been completed, press lightly on the wrong side over a well-padded surface, taking care not to crush the stitches.

Using an extremely sharp pair of embroidery scissors, cut away the background fabric from the areas indicated on the diagram. Cut as close to the buttonhole edging as you can, working slowly and carefully to avoid snipping into the embroidered areas.

EXPERIMENTING

On the traycloth, the cutwork motifs touch and slightly overlap each other, so that when the background fabric is cut away, the motifs remain joined together. To create a more lacy appearance, the motifs can be spaced slightly apart and joined by buttonholed bars or 'brides'. The bars are made at the same time as the lines of running stitch are worked. The design outlines are then covered with buttonhole stitch in the usual way and the background cut away afterwards. The sample photographed on page 23 shows a variety of bars.

brown _____

Cream - - - - - -

green ▬▬▬▬

Soft yellow ▨▨▨▨

dark orange ▬▬▬▬

light orange ▬▬▬▬

A simple buttonholed bar which you can use to join two motifs together is shown on page 49, but picots and scallops (see below) can be added to give a more ornate effect. For large, irregularly-shaped spaces, or those which fall between three or more motifs, use three or four branched bars (see below) which give an attractive lacy effect and are stronger in use than single bars. Another very decorative way of spanning a large shape is by working a ring spider's web (see below) which consists of a separately-worked buttonhole ring attached to the edges of the motifs with several plain buttonholed bars.

When working any of these bars, take care to position the ends of the foundation stitches well inside the edge which will later be cut away. This will ensure that the ends are neatly covered by the buttonhole stitches and prevent the bar from pulling the fabric out of shape on the finished article. Also, take care not to snip into a bar accidentally when cutting the ground fabric away.

Picot bar

Strand the working thread between the motifs as if you were making a plain buttonholed bar (page 49). Cover the strands with buttonhole stitch until the centre is reached, then insert a pin and make a loop around it, as shown in diagram 3. Pass the needle under the loop to secure it and bring the needle

through over the working thread. Tighten the thread, remove the pin, and complete the bar in the usual way.

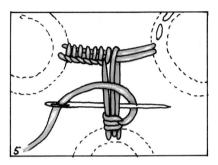

Scallop bar

Strand the working thread between the motifs as above. Cover the strands with buttonhole stitch almost to the end of the strands, then strand the working thread back and forth across the bar to make a scallop (diagram 4), ending with the working thread on the left. Cover the scallop with buttonhole stitches until the bar is reached, then complete the bar in the usual way.

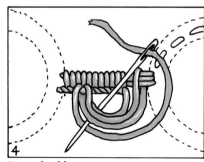

Branched bar

Strand the working thread between the motifs as above and cover with buttonhole stitch until the centre is reached, then strand the working

thread three times to and fro to join the third motif (diagram 5), and cover these strands with buttonhole stitch until the bar is reached. Complete the bar in the usual way.

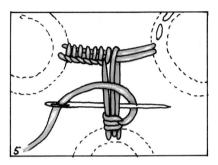

Ring spider's web

First, make a small detached ring by winding the thread six or seven times round a pencil. Slip this off, cover with buttonhole stitch and break off the thread. Darn the loose end back into the stitches and trim. Pin the ring to the fabric at the centre of the proposed space, as shown, then secure in position by working four or five buttonholed bars between the ring and the fabric. Remove the pin and cut away the fabric behind (diagram 6).

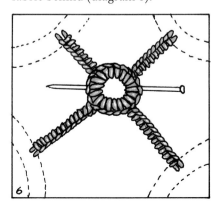

A lacy edging worked with plain buttonhole bars combined with branched bars and ring spider's webs

Enlarging a design

Enlarging a design to the correct size is quite simple to do, but remember that accurate measuring is important. Basically, you need to divide up the original design with a grid into squares of equal size, then carefully copy the design, square for square, on to a larger grid of the required size.

First, trace the design on to tracing paper. Draw a grid over the tracing, then draw in a diagonal line from bottom left to top right, as shown in diagram 1a.

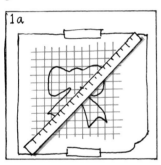

Using the diagonal line as a guide, draw a larger grid to the size required but containing the same number of squares on a separate piece of paper (diagram 1b).

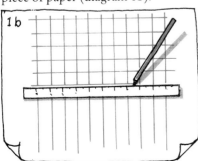

The most accurate way to copy the design is to mark the larger grid at each place where the design crosses the original grid (diagram 1c).

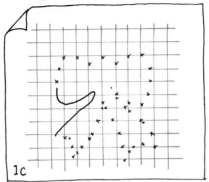

Join up these marks freehand following the original design. Once the complete design has been transferred on to the larger grid, check it back very carefully against the original (diagram 1d).

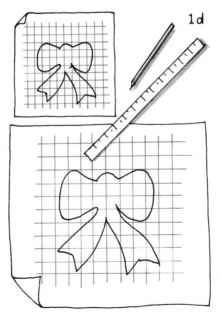

Reducing a design

To make a design smaller, follow the steps above, but this time transpose the design on to a smaller grid of the required size.

Transferring designs

Before beginning to stitch, you will need to decide how to transfer the design on to the fabric. There are several methods of doing this, depending on the type of fabric you have chosen as a background. When using plain-weave fabrics, you will need to transfer outlines as a guide to each area of embroidery. When working on an even-weave fabric, the usual method is to count the threads, following a chart to determine the placing of the stitches.

Dressmaker's carbon paper – This method works well on smooth fabrics and has the advantage of being both simple and quick. Place a sheet of dressmaker's carbon paper between the fabric and a tracing of your design. Pin the tracing in position on the fabric, keeping the pins well away from the carbon paper to avoid transferring the colour (diagram 2).

Using blue or red carbon paper for light fabrics and yellow carbon paper for dark fabrics, place the fabric on a flat, hard surface and draw round the design with a sharp, hard pencil.

Transfer pencil – This gives a result similar to a commercial transfer. Transfer pencils are available for both cotton and cotton/synthetic blends.

Trace the design on to tracing paper. Turn the tracing over and draw over the lines with the transfer pencil. Place the tracing right side up on the fabric and press with a cool iron so the lines are transferred to the fabric. When buying a transfer pencil, check that it is suitable for the composition of your fabric.

Using a light source – This method works well on finely woven, smooth fabrics.

Rest a small sheet of plate glass or perspex securely between two flat chairs and place a strong light underneath the glass, pointing upwards. A table lamp with the shade removed or an adjustable work lamp is best. Copy the design on to tracing paper and fix this to the top of the glass with strips of masking tape. Centre the fabric over the tracing, securing it with more tape. The light shining up from below will enable you to see the design through the fabric. Trace the design on to the fabric with a sharp, soft pencil (diagram 3).

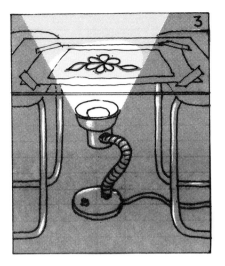

Tacking through paper – This is a good method for a simple design and has the advantage of not discolouring light fabrics.

Trace the design on to thin tracing paper (or greaseproof paper) and pin it in place on the fabric.

Tack round the traced lines with small stitches, using a fine thread in a contrasting colour. When all the tacking has been worked, tear the paper gently away from the stitches leaving the design tacked through the fabric (diagram 4). Where the embroidery does not completely hide the tacked lines, carefully remove the tacking thread with a pair of tweezers.

Prick and pounce – This is the traditional method which, although time-consuming, has the advantage of giving you a very accurate copy. Use this method for a detailed, intricate design.

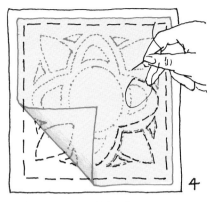

Place a tracing of the design over a thick layer of newspaper and prick along the outlines with a pin, keeping the pricked holes close together. Alternatively, stitch along the outlines with an unthreaded sewing machine (diagram 5). Pin the design right side up on the fabric. Use a small felt pad to rub pounce powder (usually powdered French chalk or charcoal, see glossary) over the holes. Remove the paper carefully, then join up the resulting dots with a fine lead or dressmaker's pencil.

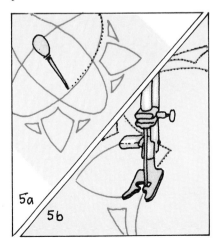

ABSTRACT PLACE SETTING

Randomly arranged abstract shapes including spots, triangles
and squares are worked in a mixture of techniques on a matching
tablemat and napkin.

Strong colours and bold shapes bring an informal place setting right up to date, providing a good contrast against plain tableware. A combination of machine zigzag stitch, hand-painted areas, and several hand embroidery stitches are used to create the design on the fabric.

You could easily adapt this design for use on a larger item, such as a tablecloth, by scattering the small abstract shapes across the surface or arranging them in regular groups at intervals round the edge. Finish the edge of the cloth by working a chevron edge (page 80) all round to echo the angular shapes of the design. ·

REQUIREMENTS

Medium weight pale grey cotton
  or polyester/cotton fabric, see
  next page for amount
Fabric paints in the following
  colours: scarlet, mid grey,
  royal blue, opaque white
Stranded cotton in the following
  colours: scarlet, mid grey,
  royal blue, white
Crewel needle sizes 6 and 7
Tacking thread

Black and grey sewing thread
Sewing needle and pins
Small embroidery hoop
Small and medium-sized
  artist's soft paintbrushes
Tracing paper
HB pencil
Thin card
Craft knife
Old newspapers
Masking tape

MEASURING UP

Rectangular tablemats in Britain usually measure about 20 by 30 cm (8 by 12 in), although they are often larger in the United States, measuring about 30 by 45 cm (12 by 18 in). To work out the right size for you, lay the table with one place setting including cutlery, glass, and two sizes of plate. Measure the area taken up and add about 5 cm (2 in) to each measurement for a border. Finally, add a hem allowance of 2.5 to 5 cm (1 to 2 in) all around.

Napkins are normally square, varying in size from small tea napkins at 30 cm (12 in) to large dinner napkins of 60 cm (24 in). To estimate the fabric for one napkin, decide on the finished size and add 1 cm (½ in) all around for hems. Bear in mind that a useful napkin size is 40 cm (16 in) square, allowing lengths of both 90 cm (36 in) and 140 cm (54 in) width fabrics to be divided evenly without wastage and allowing for hems. You will be able to cut four napkins from a 90 cm (36 in) length of 90 cm (36 in) width.

PAINTING THE MOTIFS

Cut out the fabric to the required size. Trace off the motifs which are shown actual size, then transfer each shape to the centre of a square of thin card. Carefully cut round the shape with a craft knife, discarding the central portion to leave you with a template rather like a stencil (diagram 1).

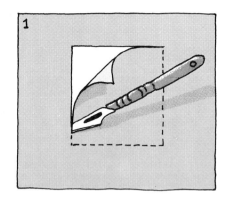

Transfer the design by placing the templates on the tablemat fabric and drawing round the inner shapes with a sharp HB pencil. Arrange the motifs at random, clustering them together in some areas. Use fewer motifs on the napkin, spacing them further apart.

For beginners to the art of fabric painting there is further information on page 70. Place each piece of fabric over a thick layer of old newspapers covered with tissue or paper towels to keep the newsprint off the fabric. Hold in position with strips of masking tape. This will prevent the fabric from moving and smearing the paint. Working with one colour at a time, outline the squares and triangles with fabric paint using the small brush.

Fill in the outlines with the larger brush. Allow to dry, then repeat with the other colours, washing the brushes out thoroughly between each colour change. Fix the paint by pressing on the wrong side following the manufacturer's instructions.

WORKING THE EMBROIDERY

Mount the fabric in the small embroidery hoop (page 16), moving it as necessary, and outline the painted squares and triangles with back stitch (page 48) using 3 strands of matching thread throughout and the size 7 crewel needle.

Fill the rectangles with satin stitch (page 56) worked on 6 strands of thread and using the size 6 crewel needle. Outline with back stitch using 3 strands of matching thread to define the edges of the shapes.

Work a ribbed spider's web (page 65) at random on the tablemat, using 3 strands of white for the straight stitches and 3 strands of scarlet or blue to work the threading. On the napkin, fill in the spots with satin stitch in 3 strands of scarlet or blue thread.

Finally, work short bars of open machine zigzag stitch with black sewing thread, scattering the bars between the other shapes.

MAKING UP

When all the embroidery has been completed, press lightly on the wrong side over a well-padded surface. Use a warm iron and take care not to flatten the stitching.

Turn up a double hem (page 72) round the edge of the tablemat and mitre the corners (page 72). Machine stitch the hem with matching thread. Press the hem.

METHOD

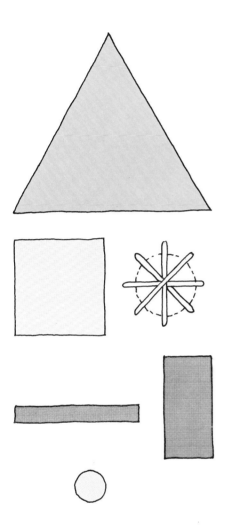

To finish the napkin, turn up a narrow double hem (page 72) round the edge, folding over the fabric neatly at the corners. Pin, tack and machine stitch with matching thread around the edge. Press the hem. Remove the tacking stitches.

FOLDING NAPKINS

First, fold the napkin in half diagonally with wrong sides facing to form a triangle. Next bring the left- and right-hand corners up to meet at the top and form a square.

Turn the napkin over so that the free edges face you. Pull the two top flaps upwards and away from you;

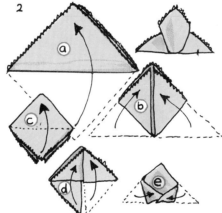

then fold the remaining flaps back in the same way to make a triangle.

Carefully turn the napkin over and overlap the two outer corners, as shown, tucking one flap into the other to hold them in place. Turn the napkin round, stand upright and gently pull down the loose flaps at each side (diagram 2).

EXPERIMENTING

Designs made by arranging small components can be easily changed to create different effects. There are several ways of doing this: by changing the scale of individual components, altering the colour scheme, or by selecting just one or two of the elements and repeating them.

Make the painted squares and triangles very large, possibly overlapping some of them, then embroider spots and rectangles of varying sizes across them so that they run on to the background. Alternatively, reduce the size of the painted areas and work the embroidery stitches on a larger scale using thicker threads, but do not have the stitches too long.

Colour schemes can drastically alter the appearance of a design. Try substituting bright pastel shades for the strong colours and scatter the shapes over a white background. For a really dramatic look, choose deep blue or green fabric and work the design in silver, bronze and gold. Metallic fabric paints are excellent and cover dark backgrounds well.

Simplify the design by selecting one or two of the shapes and repeating them in a formal arrangement – in groups, blocks or rows. Enhance the formality of the design by working it in monochrome, choosing light and dark shades of the same colour.

BREAKFAST TRAYCLOTH

Make breakfast in bed into a special occasion by serving it on a
cheerful traycloth edged with hand embroidery, woven braid
and ribbons.

Lengths of braid and ribbon decorate table linens quickly, and they are used to striking effect on this simple cotton traycloth. Group the lengths close together towards one end of the cloth and stitch them to the fabric using bright thread colours and a variety of hand embroidery stitches. The choice of ribbon and stitching will determine the overall effect. To achieve a dainty, feminine look, substitute narrow lace for the braid, choose a mixture of soft pinks, turquoises and blues and add tiny bows of matching ribbon.

REQUIREMENTS

Medium weight cream
  cotton fabric, see next
  page for amount
Short lengths of brightly-
  coloured ribbon, ric-rac
  and other braids of varying
  width

Perlé cotton size 5 in the
  following colours: yellow,
  royal blue, scarlet, green,
  purple, black
Crewel needle size 6
Tacking thread
Cream sewing thread

Sewing needle and pins
Ruler
Dressmaker's pencil
Rotating embroidery frame

METHOD

MEASURING UP

Measure the length and width of your tray and add 5 cm (2 in) to each measurement for the hem allowance.

This type of decoration also works well on a larger item, for example across two sides of a rectangular tablecloth, where the fabric joins can be hidden beneath the braid.

WORKING THE EMBROIDERY

Cut out the fabric to the required size. Lay the ribbons and braid in parallel lines across one short side of the rectangle to make a wide band, moving them around until you are satisfied with the arrangement of textures and colours. Leave narrow spaces between the lengths, so that the colour of the ground fabric shows through. Make a sketch of the arrangement, measuring the distances between the lengths carefully, then move aside.

Mount the fabric in the rotating embroidery frame (page 17), making sure the rollers are attached to the short edges of the rectangle. Tighten the lacing, so that the fabric is evenly stretched.

Mark the position of the innermost length of braid on the fabric with a dressmaker's pencil and ruler. Pin and tack this length in place, taking the stitches through the centre of the braid, not along the edges. Measure and mark the position of the next length and tack down in the same way. Repeat this sequence until all the lengths have been tacked in position.

Using diagram 1 as a stitch guide, embroider along the edges of the ribbon and braid with perlé cotton and the crewel needle. Use straight stitches and rows of blanket stitch (page 49) and fly stitch (page 64). Decorate the rows by adding individual French knots, bullion knots and daisy stitches (pages 64 and 65).

MAKING UP

When all the embroidery has been completed, remove the tacking stitches, then trim off the ribbons level with the raw edges. Press the cloth lightly on the wrong side over a well-padded surface. Press with a cool iron to suit the composition of the trimmings, since braids are often made from synthetic fibres which may be damaged by a hot iron. Take care not to crush the stitching.

Turn up a double hem (page 72) around the cloth and mitre the corners (page 72). Make sure that the upper and lower hemline folds run at right angles to the rows of ribbon and braid. Hand sew the hem with matching thread and hemming stitch (page 73), or machine stitch in place.

EXPERIMENTING

An amazing variety of ribbons and braid are widely available. Luxurious velvet ribbons in varying widths, plain and printed satins, woven tartan and alphabets, ric-rac, textured and metallic braids all come in an enormous colour range and they can be put together to create quick yet stunning trims for both formal and informal table linen.

Woven 'peasant' braids with colourful patterns of tiny houses, birds, animals and flowers can edge plain tablemats for everyday use. For a formal occasion, white damask trimmed with lengths of

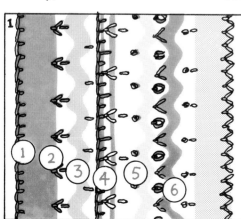

1. Blanket stitch
2. Fly stitch
3. Straight stitch
4. Long & short blanket stitch
5. French knots
6. Daisy stitch

lustrous white satin ribbon of varying widths decorated with white embroidery would make a superb covering for the dining table.

Hunt through the ribbon fixtures in a good needlecraft department, and you will probably find that many more ideas and colour combinations spring to mind.

The ribbons and braids on the traycloth have been applied using rows of hand embroidery stitches, but the effect is equally pleasing when machine stitching is used, especially when the ribbon or braid is patterned. Although a specialist machine is not essential for machine embroidery, many ordinary domestic machines can offer a range of decorative stitches controlled either manually, automatically or by a tiny internal computer.

A simple machine offering the choice of straight stitch or zigzag is surprisingly versatile, although it is a good idea to purchase a special embroidery foot. This is wider than the normal sewing foot and has an open area to let you see the stitches as they are being worked. Some manufacturers can supply a clear plastic embroidery foot which is excellent. Use machine embroidery threads which are finer than standard sewing threads and come in a range of solid and shaded colours, plus shiny metallics. They are also available in different thicknesses.

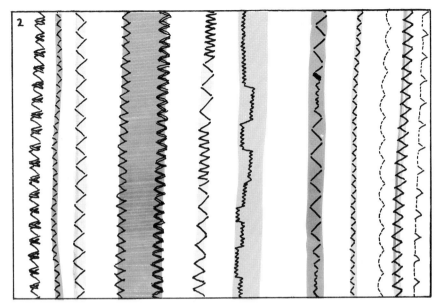

Work several practice pieces before starting on a particular project. At first, try out simple variations of zigzag by stitching in straight rows and altering the width and stitch length from widely-spaced open zigzag to close satin stitch. Next watch the effect of changing the stitch width sharply or gradually on the same row. If you can alter the needle position on your particular machine easily, try working blocks of satin stitch in each needle position and alternating the blocks along the row (diagram 2).

In addition, owners of sophisticated machines could try out their full range of stitch patterns using different types of thread. Number the rows and note down width and stitch length for each row as you go. Should your fabric begin to pucker, place a piece of thin typing paper beneath the area you are stitching and tear it away later.

When you have practised these exercises several times and feel confident handling your machine, prepare a sample by tacking down parallel lengths of ribbon and braid on to a piece of medium weight cotton fabric, then try out all the stitch variations you have been practising.

Stitch down both edges of the ribbon or braid, work one wide row of stitching down the centre or take the stitches right across narrow ribbon and into the fabric at either side. At the end of each row of stitching, leave a long thread on the right side. When all the embroidery has been completed, pull the threads through to the wrong side, knot them in pairs and trim off the ends.

EVEN-WEAVE NAPKINS

Stitch a set of even-weave napkins to coordinate with a plain or contrasting tablecloth and trim each of them with a geometric motif in cross stitch.

Even-weave fabric makes a good background for cross stitch embroidery. The weave allows you to work cross stitches of identical size and shape in the same way as fabric which is printed or woven with a regular pattern of spots, stripes or checks.

Napkins are quick and simple to make using several colourways of even-weave cotton or linen fabric. Decorate each napkin with a geometric motif worked from the chart. To show off your napkins, make a matching tablecloth or set of quilted tablemats.

REQUIREMENTS

Lightweight cotton or linen 12-count even-weave fabric 90 cm (36 in) wide, in dark colours, see next page for length
Stranded cotton in the following colours: yellow, orange, light green, mid green

Tapestry needle size 22
Tacking thread
Matching sewing threads
Sewing needle and pins
Small embroidery hoop

MEASURING UP

Traditionally, napkins are square, varying in size from dainty tea napkins of 30 cm (12 in) to large dinner napkins of 60 cm (24 in). To estimate the fabric for one napkin, decide on the finished size and add 1 cm (½ in) all around for hems.

However, a good all-purpose size for a napkin is 40 cm (16 in) square as lengths of both 90 cm (36 in) and 140 cm (54 in) width fabrics can be divided evenly for napkins of this size with sufficient for hem allowances without wastage. From a 90 cm (36 in) length of fabric you will be able to cut four napkins from 90 cm (36 in) width fabric and six from 140 cm (54 in) fabric.

WORKING THE EMBROIDERY

Cut out the fabric to the required size. Mark the position of the base of the motif with pins approximately 7.5 cm (3 in) from the corner, then mount the corner of one piece of fabric in the small embroidery hoop (page 16).

Begin working the first motif from the chart in cross stitch (right), using the chosen colours, with 6 strands of thread in the tapestry needle throughout. Each square on the chart represents one cross stitch worked over one woven fabric block.

Work a different motif at the corner of each square of fabric, using the colours indicated in the list on the previous page.

MAKING UP

When all the embroidery has been completed, press the napkins lightly on the wrong side over a well-padded surface with a warm iron, taking care not to flatten the embroidery.

Turn up a narrow double hem (page 72) round each napkin, folding over the fabric neatly at the corners. Pin, tack and machine stitch with matching thread around the edge. Press the hem. Remove the tacking stitches.

EXPERIMENTING

A selection of cross stitch motifs forms a useful design resource for the embroiderer. Motifs are enormously versatile, as they can be worked singly to decorate a napkin, or grouped in blocks or arranged side by side to form an ornate border for a large cloth for the dining table.

Working the same motif on a larger or smaller scale in varying weights of thread and on different fabrics can totally change its appearance.

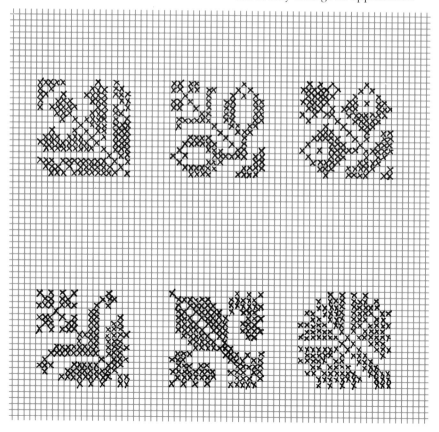

Designing a cross stitch monogram

In addition to geometric designs, simple floral motifs and letters can be combined to make an attractive monogram, adding an individual touch to many items of table linen. Shown here is a simple alphabet and a selection of small flower shapes, both charted for cross stitch.

Choose the appropriate initials from the alphabet and try out various ways of combining them into a single device. Trace the letters one after the other, allowing the second initial to overlap or interlock with the first. Add a third and fourth letter if required, altering the position of the letters until you get a pleasing arrangement.

One of the simplest ways to create a well-balanced monogram is to line up the vertical strokes of two letters, for example H and E, or you could position a narrow J on top of a wide E. Graph tracing paper (tracing paper with a ready-printed grid), if obtainable, will simplify this stage considerably.

Alternatively, copy the letters square by square on to ordinary graph paper.

When you are satisfied with the arrangement of the initials, consider adding one or more floral motifs as decoration. Position mirror images of the same flower at each side of your monogram, or join several tiny flowers together and create a curved garland below the letters. At this stage, draw a neat copy of the monogram on graph paper and chart in the colours before beginning to stitch the design.

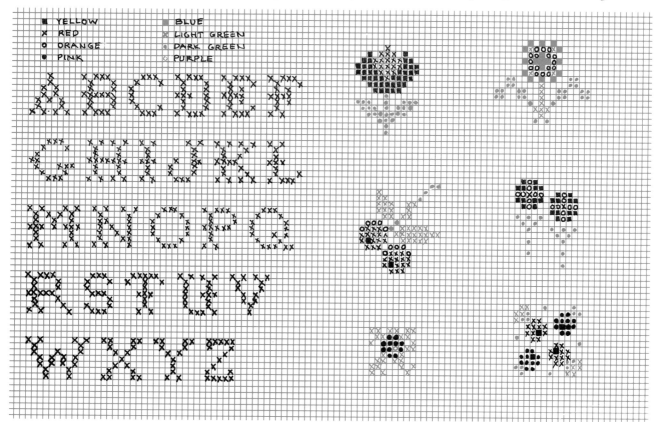

APPLIQUÉ TABLECLOTH

A garland of flower shapes cut from printed fabric
and applied with blanket stitch decorates
this extravagant circular tablecloth.

Make the tablecloth short or right down to the floor, depending on your preference, and apply cut-out motifs to make a deep band just below the edge of the table. To add more decoration, scatter smaller individual motifs across the top of the cloth. Choose the printed fabric carefully, selecting one which has a bold, well-defined pattern of flower shapes which are easy to cut out. You may be lucky enough to find two fabrics printed with coordinating motifs in graduated sizes. Matching tablemats could be made if the flower shapes are sufficiently large. To make flower-shaped tablemats, sandwich a layer of heavy non-woven interfacing between a cut-out motif and backing fabric. Tack together, then stitch round the edge with buttonhole stitch. Cut away the excess fabric and remove tacking.

REQUIREMENTS

Medium weight cream
   cotton fabric, see next
   page for amount
Medium weight printed
   cotton with a large floral
   pattern in coordinating
   colours

Iron-on bonding web
Cream stranded cotton
Crewel needle size 7
Tacking thread
Cream sewing thread
Sewing needle and pins
Bias binding (optional)

Large embroidery hoop
Drawing pin
Pencil
Length of fine string
Dressmaker's pattern paper

MEASURING UP

Measure the diameter of the table top, then decide how far the cloth will hang down over the edge of the table. When making a short cloth, measure from the top of the table to a chair seat; for a long cloth, measure right down to the floor. Multiply this measurement by two and add to the diameter of the table. Finally, add twice the hem allowance of 1.5 cm (⅝ in).

Where the diameter of the cloth is less than the width of your chosen fabric, one length of fabric will be sufficient. When the diameter is wider, you will need to join two or more fabric widths together.

Do this by joining strips of fabric to both sides of a central panel. Cut one piece of fabric to the same length as the diameter of the tablecloth. Cut the remaining fabric in half lengthwise and join one strip to each side of the first length to make a square, matching the selvages to make neat seams.

Join the strips together with a plain seam (page 81), taking a 1.5 cm (⅝ in) seam allowance. Press the seams open.

CUTTING OUT

Fold the square of fabric in half with right sides facing, then fold in half again to make a square. Mark the corner which is formed at the centre of the fabric with three or four tacking stitches.

Make a paper pattern by first cutting a square of dressmaker's pattern paper to the same size as the folded fabric. Take a piece of string. Tie one end of the string round a drawing pin and the other end round a pencil. The distance between the pin and the pencil should equal half the diameter of the tablecloth. Place the pin in corner A of the paper and, holding the pencil at right angles to the paper, draw an arc from B to C, as shown in diagram 1. Cut out the paper pattern.

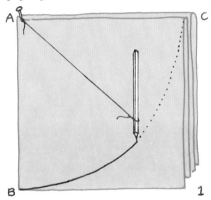

Lay the pattern on top of the folded fabric, making sure that corner A is lying exactly over the tacked corner. Pin the pattern to the fabric and cut out along the curved line. Remove the tacking stitches and open out the cloth. Keep the paper pattern for future use.

WORKING THE EMBROIDERY

Pick out a selection of floral motifs from the printed fabric and cut them out roughly, leaving a margin of at least 2.5 cm (1 in) all round. Cut pieces of bonding web to the same size and shape, place on the wrong side of the motifs with the backing paper uppermost and press with a warm, dry iron. Leave to cool.

Trim round the motifs carefully with a pair of sharp scissors, leaving a 3 mm (⅛ in) margin round the edge of each shape. You may need to simplify complex flowers slightly to give a pleasantly curving outline.

Lay the motifs round the cloth to make a garland just below the edge of the table, overlapping the shapes as necessary. Pin all the motifs in position, then try the cloth on the table to check the arrangement. Make any adjustments at this point.

Mark the position of the first motif with several pins. Remove the motif and peel off the backing paper. Replace in position on the cloth, cover with a damp cloth and press with a hot, dry iron. Leave to cool. Repeat with each motif.

N.B. *Should you prefer not to use bonding web, tack the motifs securely in position instead.*

Mount the fabric in the large embroidery hoop (page 16), moving it as necessary. Using 3 strands of embroidery thread in the crewel needle, embroider round the edge of the motifs with a row of blanket stitches (page 49). Keep the stitches quite close together, and space them evenly along the edge of the motifs. If tacking threads have been used, remove any that show once the embroidery is completed.

MAKING UP

When all the motifs have been applied, press lightly on the wrong side over a well-padded surface with a warm iron.

Make a narrow hem round the cloth with matching thread as described on page 72, or bind the edge with bias binding as shown on page 73, second method. Press the hem.

EXPERIMENTING

Appliqué with printed fabrics is great fun and the whole process can be speeded up considerably by applying the motifs with satin stitch worked by machine instead of the hand-embroidered blanket stitch. Prepare the motifs in the same way, set your machine to zigzag stitch and carefully satin stitch round each flower motif to completely cover the raw edges. Practise on pieces of spare fabric first, as you may need to adjust the length and spacing of the stitches to achieve a satisfactory result. You could also design your own flower shapes and cut these out of plain or small-patterned fabric.

To make a stunning overcloth for a round occasional table, cut out a square of plain fabric about 40 cm

(16 in) larger than the table top. Cut out large floral motifs from printed fabric and tack them around the square, so that they project over the edge. Cut four strips of lightweight non-woven interfacing as a backing for the outside flowers and tack them in place, overlapping the raw edges of the fabric square (diagram 2). Tack the lower edges of the motifs to the interfacing, then satin stitch round the motifs as described above. Finally, cut the interfacing carefully away close to the stitching.

Investigate the possibilities of using different types of prints. Geometric designs, for instance, can often be cut out and rearranged to great effect, enhanced by the use of two or three colourways of the same design. Children's furnishing fabrics often feature bold, colourful prints of toys, animals or spaceships. These can be cut out and applied to a brightly coloured background to make a wonderful birthday tea cloth.

Cut out chunky numbers and letters from contrasting plain fabric and apply these in the same way.

HERRINGBONE TABLECLOTH

Worked on even-weave fabric, this stylish tablecloth
features decorative hem stitching and a graphic arrangement of
three types of herringbone stitches.

Fabric threads are withdrawn and the remaining threads grouped in clusters with hem stitches to create an attractive edge on this linen cloth. Hem stitches are also used to work the two bands which divide the surface of the cloth into quarters. Inside each quarter, narrow blocks of ordinary herringbone stitch and two attractive threaded variations are worked above the hem.

Traditionally worked in a matching fabric and thread colour, hem stitches are also very effective when worked in a bright contrasting colour, although the appearance is less delicate. Narrower bands are achieved by withdrawing fewer threads. For a different effect, work further crossing bands of hem stitch to divide the cloth into smaller areas and keep the blocks of herringbone stitch quite small.

REQUIREMENTS

Cream even-weave linen:
choose one with a loose
weave, so that the threads
can be easily withdrawn,
see next page for quantity
Perlé cotton size 5 and
stranded cotton in the
following colours: cream,
green, gold, pink, light
blue, mid blue, turquoise
Tapestry needle size 22
Tacking thread in a dark
colour
Cream sewing thread
Sewing needle and pins
Medium embroidery hoop

MEASURING UP

The cloth shown in the photograph measures 1 m (39 in) square and is made from a loosely-woven linen with an even weave. Although this type of fabric is available in several different widths, the fabric you select will limit the size of the finished cloth as this design will not be successful worked on fabric which has been joined.

Keeping this in mind, should you wish to make the cloth rectangular rather than square, measure up in the following way. First measure the length and width of the table top; decide how far the cloth will hang down over the edge of the table and add twice this measurement to each of the table top measurements. Finally, add 5 cm (2 in) to each measurement for the hem allowance.

When working the embroidery on a rectangular cloth, work more blocks of herringbone stitches down the two long sides. For a smaller cloth, work fewer blocks of stitches.

PREPARING THE FABRIC

To prepare the fabric for embroidery, you must first remove some of the fabric threads and tack the hem in position ready for the hem stitches to be worked.

Cut out the fabric to the required size. Measure 5 cm (2 in) in from the raw edge and mark each corner with a pin. This pin denotes the outer corner of the hem stitched border. Begin at one corner and run a line of tacking stitches right round the fabric, working from pin to pin, and being careful not to cross any horizontal threads (diagram 1).

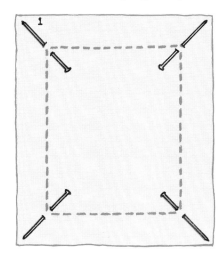

Working inside the tacked line, cut three fabric threads about 7.5 cm (3 in) away from the corner points, then withdraw the centre portions to leave the loose ends, as shown (diagram 2). When working on a fine fabric, you may need to withdraw more than three threads in order to work the hem stitches. Remove the tacking. Repeat round the other three sides.

Working in the same way, cut three threads about 5 cm (2 in) in from the midpoint of one side of the border. Run a line of tacking to the opposite side, then cut the three corresponding threads about 5 cm (2 in) in from the border. Withdraw

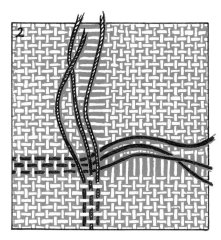

the threads as above. Repeat on the other two sides. Remove the tacking.

To finish off the loose ends, cut them off close to the edge and secure the raw edge with buttonhole stitch (page 49) worked in cream perlé cotton. Alternatively, trim the ends to 1 cm (½ in), fold them back to the wrong side and tack in position so they can be secured under the hem (diagram 3).

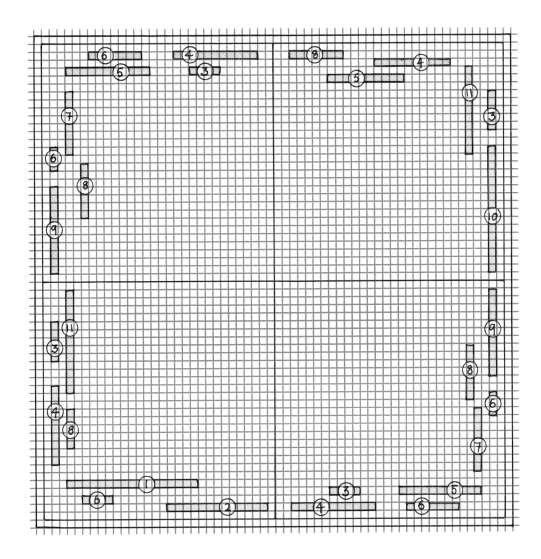

Stitch and colour key

1 Blue herringbone stitch threaded with pink
2 Green herringbone stitch interlaced with light orange
3 Lavender herringbone stitch
4 Light yellow herringbone stitch threaded with turquoise
5 Turquoise herringbone stitch interlaced with royal blue
6 Green herringbone stitch
7 Green herringbone stitch threaded with pink
8 Royal blue herringbone stitch
9 Light yellow herringbone stitch
interlaced with lavender
10 Light blue herringbone stitch threaded with pink
11 Green herringbone stitch interlaced with turquoise

Fold over 6 mm (¼ in) of the raw edge to the wrong side and press. Turn up the hem, so that the fold lies along the lower edge of the drawn threads and press. Mitre the corners using the first method described on page 72, slipstitch (page 73) the corners with matching sewing thread, then tack the hem accurately in position.

WORKING THE EMBROIDERY

Work either hem stitch or antique hem stitch (pages 80 and 81) in cream perlé cotton to secure the hem, depending on the effect preferred.

Work hem stitch along each edge of the two crossing bands of withdrawn threads, grouping identical clusters of threads together, creating a 'ladder' of threads (diagram 4).

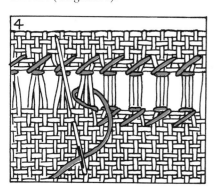

Mount the fabric in the embroidery hoop (page 16) and, using the tapestry needle, work narrow blocks of herringbone stitch, threaded herringbone stitch and interlaced herringbone stitch (page 57) in perlé and stranded cotton, following the colour, size and position indicated on the diagram (page 45).

MAKING UP

When all the embroidery has been completed, press lightly on the wrong side over a well-padded surface. Use a warm iron and take care not to press too hard and crush the stitching.

Finally, remove the tacking round the hem and press the edge of the hem with a hot iron to make a crisp fold.

EXPERIMENTING

The many forms of herringbone stitch, like cross stitch and its variations, give the best results when worked on even-weave fabrics. However, this does not mean there is no scope for further experiments with these counted thread stitches.

Simply by altering the scale of the stitches, you can change the effect of a design considerably. For example, suppose you were working cross stitch (page 56) on Aida fabric which has the fabric threads woven into neat blocks. You could work each stitch in the usual manner over one block of threads, or over four blocks or more to make the stitches and the resulting design larger. Changing the fabric gauge will also alter the size of the stitches.

However, by working each cross stitch over a rectangular area, such as two blocks wide and four blocks deep, you can distort the design to make it long and narrow. Similarly, by working each stitch of the identical design over a rectangle two blocks wide and one deep you will achieve a completely different distortion.

The appearance of herringbone stitches can be varied by changing both the spacing of the stitches and the depth of the band being worked. Try arranging the stitches so that they touch at the top and bottom of the row, then spread them widely apart and alter the depth of the row.

Substituting different threads can be fun when working the two herringbone variations on page 57. Stitch the foundation row of ordinary herringbone stitches using a thick, heavy thread and work the threading or interlacing in a fine metallic thread, then change over the threads to work the next row. All kinds of threads including knitting yarns, tapestry wool and fine cord give interesting results when used for threading and interlacing, but you may need to make the herringbone stitches quite large to accommodate these threads. Slubbed and slightly textured threads also work well, but avoid those textured with large knots and bobbles as they are almost impossible to pull through the foundation row without dragging the stitches out of shape.

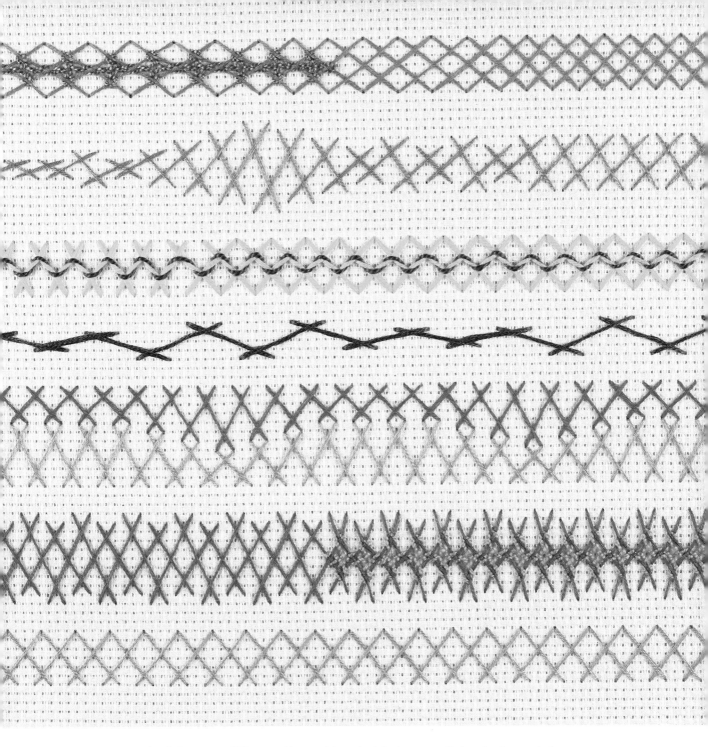

A sample of the many different effects achieved with the versatile herringbone stitch

Left-handed working

For a left-handed worker, the diagrams will be easier to follow if you first prop the book up in front of a mirror, then follow the reflected images.

Running stitch

The most basic of all stitches, running stitch is quick and simple to work. It has several uses: to work outlines and details in small areas on both plain- and even-weave fabrics, to create a light filling stitch when stitched in multiple rows, to outline shapes in hand quilting and as a strengthening stitch in cutwork.

Work running stitch from right to left, taking the needle in and out of the fabric at regular intervals. You can work this stitch evenly by picking up two or three fabric threads between each stitch. Alternatively, vary the spaces between the stitches for a less formal effect.

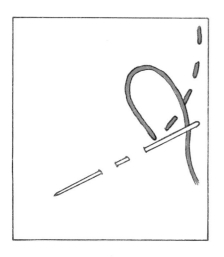

Back stitch

Back stitch is one of the most useful outline stitches as it is suitable for complicated as well as simple shapes. When worked with small, neat stitches, it produces a delicate line rather like machine stitching. Use this stitch on both plain- and even-weave fabrics.

Work back stitch from right to left, as shown, working the stitches forwards and backwards along the line. Keep the stitches small and regular, placing them close together to make a solid line of stitching.

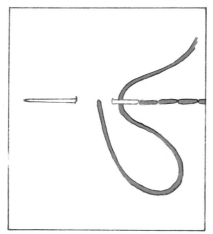

Stem stitch

Stem stitch is popular for working intricate naturalistic designs on plain-weave fabrics. It is quick and easy to work, producing a neat, raised line which has a slightly heavier appearance than a back stitched line.

Work stem stitch upwards with a forwards and backwards motion, insert the needle directly into the line being stitched and bring it up again along the same line. Alternatively, produce a wider line by inserting the needle into the fabric at a slight angle and to one side of the stitch line. Keep the working thread to the right of the needle and make all the stitches of equal size.

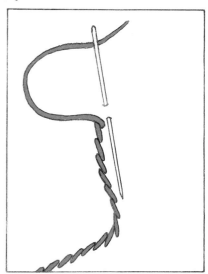

Chain stitch

Chain stitch is a very old embroidery stitch and examples of it can be found decorating antique and contemporary textiles throughout the world. Simple to work, it makes an excellent outline or filling stitch on both plain- and even-weave fabrics. To fill a shape, work this stitch in multiple rows.

Work chain stitch downwards, as shown, by making a series of loops of identical size. Catch down the last loop on to the fabric with a tiny straight stitch.

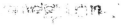

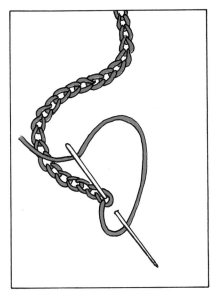

Blanket stitch

Both blanket stitch and buttonhole stitch (below) are worked in the same way, but the stitches are spaced differently. Blanket stitch is used as a surface stitch on plain- and even-weave fabrics and as an edging for appliqué. It makes a wide, decorative line which is suitable for outlining both curved and straight shapes. Vary the effect by making the upright stitches alternately long and short.

Work blanket stitch from left to right, taking the needle through the fabric at right angles to the line and pulling it out over the working thread to form a loop.

Buttonhole stitch

Buttonhole stitch, as the name suggests, can be used to work buttonholes but also creates a decorative edge finish for many types of embroidery, including cutwork.

Work from left to right in the same way as blanket stitch (above), but position the stitches close together so that no ground fabric shows through the stitching.

When embroidering cutwork, the same stitch is also used to make buttonholed bars. These are worked at the same time as the outlining of the motifs. Work round the outline using running stitch (above) until the position for one end of the bar is reached. At this point strand the working thread to the other end of the bar three times to and fro. Cover the strands with buttonhole stitch, then continue to outline the motif until the position of the next bar is reached.

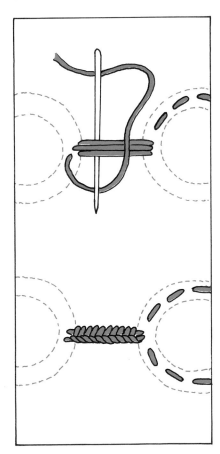

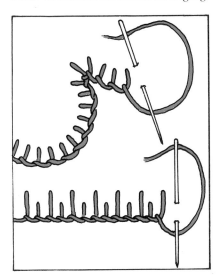

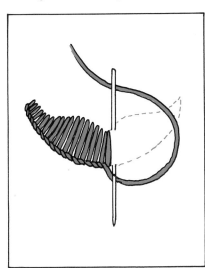

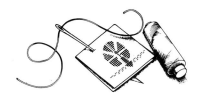

CROSS STITCH TABLECLOTH

Perfect for afternoon tea, this square cloth is decorated with
twining stems, leaves and roses stitched in delicate shades of
purple, lavender and green.

Cross stitch embroidery has an innate charm
and freshness all of its own, and there have
been a wealth of lovely patterns created
especially for this stitch both traditional and
modern. Embroider this charming, old-
fashioned border around each edge of your
cloth, or just stitch the corner motifs for a
simpler effect. Complement the cloth with a
set of matching napkins decorated with single
flower motifs. For an edge finish with a more
decorative appearance, substitute the hem
stitched edge described on page 80.

REQUIREMENTS

White even-weave cotton
  fabric woven in blocks,
  e.g. Aida, with a gauge of
  12 blocks to 2.5 cm (1 in),
  see next page for amount
Stranded cotton in the
  following colours:
  lavender, shaded purple,
  mid green, shaded green

Tapestry needle size 24
Tacking thread in a dark
  colour
White sewing thread
Sewing needle and pins
Large embroidery hoop

MEASURING UP

The embroidery was designed to fit a small afternoon tea cloth 96 cm (38 in) square. If you prefer to make a larger cloth to fit a rectangular table, for example, first measure the length and width of the table top, then decide how far the cloth will hang down over the edge of the table and add twice this measurement to each of the table top measurements. Finally, add 5 cm (2 in) to each measurement for the hem allowance (diagram 1).

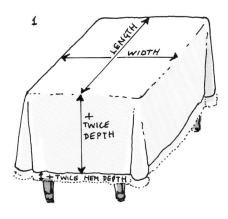

When working the embroidery, extend the length of the border to suit the dimensions of your cloth by working more border sections along each side, making sure there is enough space to work whole sections. For a smaller cloth, shorten the border by working fewer sections.

Remember that even-weave fabric is available in different widths, depending on which type you

choose. The fabric width will limit the size you can make the finished cloth as this design will not be successful worked on fabric which has been joined.

WORKING THE EMBROIDERY

Cut out the fabric to the required size. Tack a vertical line through the centre of the fabric, taking care not to cross any vertical threads. Mark the central horizontal line in the same way. Along one side tack a guideline 15 cm (6 in) in from the raw edge of the fabric (diagram 2).

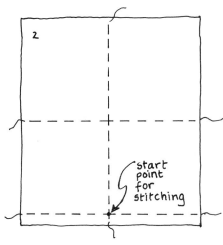

Begin working the embroidery at the centre of this side, noting that the tacked line represents the lower edge of the chart. Mount the fabric in the large embroidery hoop (page 16), moving it as necessary. Work with 3 strands of thread in the tapestry needle throughout. Remember that each square on the chart represents one stitch, and each

cross stitch covers 4 woven fabric blocks. Embroider the stems and leaves in cross stitch (page 56) from the border chart, using green thread as indicated. Complete the section by stitching the flowers and buds in the same way, using the colours indicated on the chart.

Working towards the corner from the completed border section, repeat the border chart until the position for the corner motif is reached, then embroider the corner section shown in the second chart. At this point, check over your embroidery, making sure that each flower and leaf motif is complete, and that the base of the border runs along the tacked line.

Tack a guideline from the completed corner along the adjacent side of the fabric towards the second corner. Embroider along this side, repeating the border chart to match the first side. Embroider the second corner and repeat the process around the cloth.

MAKING UP

When all the embroidery has been completed, remove the tacking threads, then press the cloth lightly on the wrong side over a well-padded surface. Use a warm iron and take care not to press too hard, which would crush the stitching. Turn up a double hem (page 72) round the cloth and mitre the corners (page 72). Make sure that the hemline fold runs neatly between two rows of fabric blocks

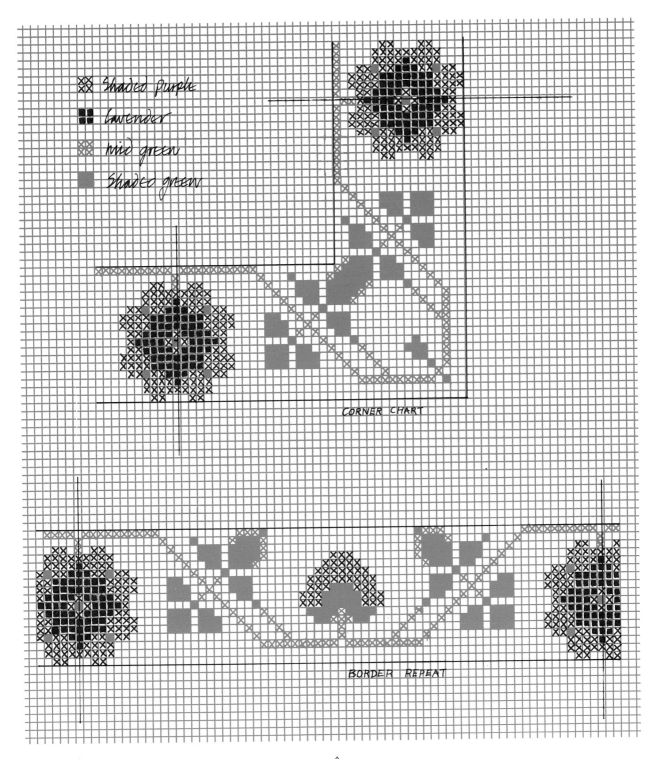

Shaded purple

Lavender

mid green

Shaded green

CORNER CHART

BORDER REPEAT

(diagram 3) and also that the embroidered border is an equal distance from the hem edge at each side. Hand sew the hem with matching thread and hemming stitch (page 73).

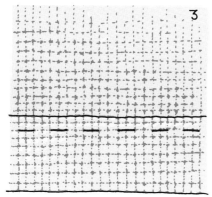

To complete the cloth, work a row of spaced single cross stitches in lavender just above the hem, as shown in the photograph. Press the edge of the hem with a hot iron to make a crisp fold.

EXPERIMENTING

Cross stitch borders

There are various ways of creating a cross stitch border pattern. Two or three rows of cross stitch in different colours form solid stripes, or the colours can be changed at regular intervals to make an alternating chequered pattern. Narrow geometric borders three or four stitches in depth can be repeated across the fabric in multiple rows, building up into a richly-patterned band of solid embroidery. Sketch out your ideas on graph paper, using coloured pencils or pens to indicate the colours, before stitching a small sample to gauge the effect.

Many borders feature simple geometric motifs repeated at regular intervals along the strip, and a one-way design can be turned at the centre of the border to add interest. Look at traditional Fair Isle knitting patterns for inspiration, as these are usually already charted and easy to adapt for cross stitch.

Pictorial motifs make unusual borders. Repeat the motifs in rows or position them face to face in pairs with one motif reversed. Twining borders, inspired by old sampler designs, are among the most complicated to construct as they consist of a basic stem travelling from top to bottom of the border strip at regular intervals. The length of each section has to be carefully calculated to accommodate various motifs and several adjustments may be necessary before you are happy with the final result (see samples in diagram 4).

Colour also plays an important part in designing a cross stitch border. The design can be monochrome, or you could use a selection of different colours. Try working the same design using several colour combinations: shades of grey, bright colours or subtle pastels, for example. You can leave the background fabric unstitched, or fill it in completely with a contrasting colour. Alternatively, work the embroidery in just one colour, leaving the design unstitched and filling in the background.

Consider what will happen at the corners when you want to use a border to frame a tablecloth or tablemat. You can work the border as four distinct sections along the sides, leaving the corner unstitched, or incorporate a motif or separate block of pattern to break the sequence of the strip.

The neatest way to turn the corner is by using a small mirror to reverse the border and turn the design at a 45° angle. To do this, draw out a section of your border pattern on to graph paper. Stand a small mirror on its edge across the design, setting it at an angle of approximately 45° to the top of the border. A reverse image of the border will appear in the mirror, then you can chart the intersection on graph paper (diagram 5). You may need to move the mirror along the design to different points before a pleasing image appears.

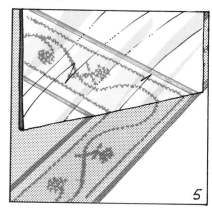

Satin stitch

Satin stitch is a smooth filling stitch which, in spite of looking easy to work, needs some practice to achieve a neat and regular effect. Work this stitch on either plain- or even-weave fabric mounted in an embroidery hoop to prevent puckering.

Work each stitch by taking the working thread right across the shape, returning it beneath the fabric close to the point where it emerged. Place the stitches close together and keep an even tension on the thread. Long satin stitches tend to become loose and untidy, so split up large shapes into small sections or work them in long and short stitch for a similar effect.

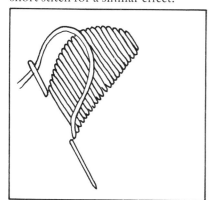

Long and short stitch

Long and short stitch is a filling stitch which is worked in a similar way to satin stitch (above), and is used to cover large areas. Its particular attraction is that it allows areas of colour to blend gradually into one another. Work on fabric mounted in an embroidery hoop.

Begin by making a foundation row of alternately long and short satin stitches round the edge of the shape. Keep the stitches close together so that the ground fabric is well covered. On the next row, fit satin stitches of equal length into the spaces left in the foundation row. Continue in this way until the shape is covered.

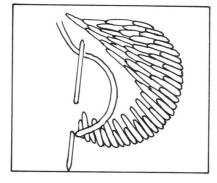

Cross stitch

Cross stitch is thought to be the oldest known embroidery stitch. Simple to work, it is mainly used on even-weave fabrics where the threads can be counted to keep the stitches of equal shape and size. It can be used as an outline or border stitch or as a filling stitch for complete motifs. To work cross stitch successfully on plain-weave fabrics, choose one with a regular pattern of spots or checks.

There are two methods of working cross stitch. In both the top diagonals should all fall in the same direction. The first diagram shows how to work cross stitch on plain-weave fabric over two journeys. First work a row of diagonal

stitches from right to left, then cross them with a second row of diagonal stitches on the return journey.

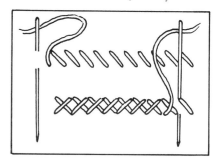

The second method is used on even-weave fabrics to give an even tension to the stitching. Each row requires four journeys to complete the crosses. On the first journey, working from right to left, stitch every alternate diagonal stitch along the row. Complete these diagonals on the second journey, working from left to right. To finish, work the top diagonals over two more journeys, as shown.

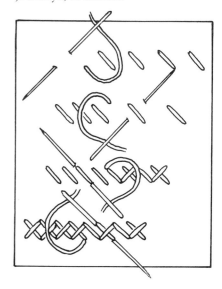

Herringbone stitch

Herringbone stitch is a border stitch used on both plain- and even-weave fabrics. It is worked in straight rows from left to right. To execute this stitch neatly and evenly, choose an even-weave fabric or mark parallel guidelines on plain-weave fabric with a dressmaker's pencil.

Begin at the left of the row. Bring the needle through the fabric on the top guideline, then make a short stitch from right to left a little further along the lower line. Make a second short stitch along the top line, spacing the stitches evenly as shown. Repeat along the line.

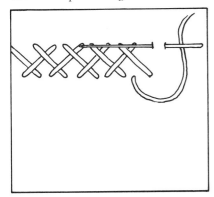

Threaded herringbone stitch

Threaded herringbone stitch makes a narrow, decorative border on both plain- and even-weave fabrics. It is usually worked in two thread colours, and a tapestry needle should be used for the second stage. To work the foundation row neatly, choose an even-weave fabric or mark parallel guidelines on plain-weave fabric with a dressmaker's pencil.

Begin with a row of herringbone stitches (above), then work the lacing from left to right, taking the second thread over and under the foundation stitches, as shown. The lacing is worked on the right side of the fabric without picking up any fabric threads. Bring the second thread through the fabric only at the beginning and end of each row.

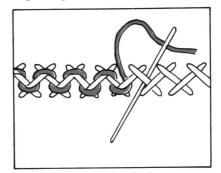

Interlaced herringbone stitch

Interlaced herringbone stitch produces a wide, interlaced border on both plain- and even-weave fabrics. The lacing thread should be thick enough to fill the centre spaces between the foundation stitches. Choose an even-weave fabric, or mark guidelines on plain-weave with a dressmaker's pencil. Stretch the fabric in an embroidery hoop to enable the stitches to be worked evenly. As with threaded herringbone stitch (above), it is usually worked in two colours of thread.

Work a row of loose herringbone stitches (above), then complete the foundation by working a second row over the top, as shown. Check that the sequence of 'unders' and 'overs' is correct, then work the interlacing over two journeys. The interlacing is worked on the right side of the fabric, using a tapestry needle, without picking up any fabric threads. Bring the thread through the fabric and work the interlacing along the top of the foundation row, as shown. Take the thread round the central cross at the end, then return in the opposite direction to complete.

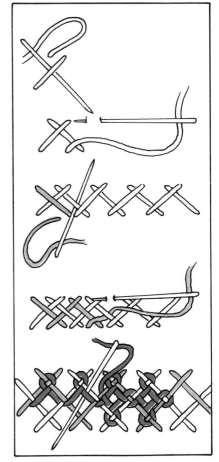

QUILTED TABLEMAT

Quilt a design of stylized flowers and leaves to make a set of
unusual heat-resisting tablemats. Add decorative touches with
embroidery stitches.

The familiar padded quilting, also known as
English quilting, is worked by stitching along
the outline of a design with running stitch or
back stitch, taking the needle right through
three layers of fabric and wadding. The layer
of wadding is sandwiched between top and
backing fabrics, then carefully tacked in
position so that quilting stitches can be worked
in the hand without a frame. Quilting is an
ideal technique to use for making tablemats as
the resulting fabric not only looks attractive
but will also protect your table from warm
plates and dishes. However, do not place
dishes taken straight from the oven on to a
fabric tablemat; use a thick cork mat or
wooden trivet instead.

REQUIREMENTS

Closely-woven yellow cotton
   fabric, see next page for
   amount
Lightweight (2 oz) polyester
   wadding, see next page
   for amount

Lightweight cotton backing
   fabric in a matching or
   contrasting colour, see
   next page for amount
Yellow coton à broder
Stranded cotton in the
   following colours: pale
   blue, mid blue, light green,
   orange

Crewel needle sizes 6 and 7
Tacking thread
Yellow sewing thread
Yellow bias binding 25 mm
   (1 in) wide
Sewing needle and pins
Tracing paper

MEASURING UP

Traditionally in Britain, tablemats are rectangular, measuring approximately 20 by 30 cm (8 by 12 in), or circular measuring between 20 and 25 cm (8 and 10 in) in diameter. Tablemats are usually larger in the United States, approximately 30 by 45 cm (12 by 18 in) or between 30 and 38 cm (12 and 15 in) in diameter.

To decide the best size for your table, lay out a standard place setting including cutlery, glass, and two sizes of plate. Measure the area used and add about 5 cm (2 in) all round for a border. Allow an extra 5 cm (2 in) all round when cutting out both pieces of fabric and the wadding. The surplus will be cut away after the stitching has been completed.

PREPARING THE FABRIC

Cut out the fabrics and wadding to the required size. Trace and enlarge the design (page 61) to the required dimensions. Transfer the design to the top fabric using one of the methods described on page 24.

Place the backing fabric right side down on a flat surface, smoothing it out to remove any wrinkles. Lay the wadding on top, then place the top fabric right side up on top of the other two layers.

Work large tacking stitches horizontally and vertically across the surface starting at the centre and working outwards in each direction, smoothing the fabric to prevent wrinkling. To avoid knots in the tacking thread which, during removal, may catch and snag in the quilting stitches, work each row in

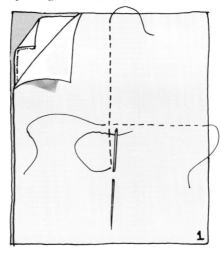

this way: starting at the centre, leave half the length of tacking thread free on the surface (diagram 1). Tack the first half of the row, then rethread the needle and complete the other half of the row.

When all the horizontal and vertical lines of tacking have been completed, finish by tacking diagonal lines from corner to corner.

WORKING THE QUILTING

Begin at the centre of the design. Thread the crewel needle size 7 with a short length of yellow cotan à broder and make a small knot at the end. Insert the needle through the layers from the underside and pull the knot through the backing fabric, so that it lies in the wadding.

Work the quilting lines in running stitches (page 48) and back stitches (page 48), as indicated on the design.

To finish off each length of thread, make a small back stitch on the wrong side and knot the thread close to the fabric. Slide the needle through the backing and wadding far enough to hide the knot when pulled through. Bring the needle out on the right side a short distance from the line of stitching and cut off the thread close to the fabric. Work the cut end through to the inside by sliding the point of the needle under the top fabric and thread.

When all the quilting has been completed, carefully remove all the tacking stitches.

WORKING THE EMBROIDERY

Using the size 6 crewel needle, work French knots (page 64) and bullion knots (page 65) in 6 strands of blue and orange stranded cotton at the centres of the flowers as indicated on the design.

Dot small French knots worked in 3 strands of green thread at random at the base of the leaf shapes.

_____ back stitch

------ running stitch

MAKING UP

Do not press the finished embroidery unless absolutely necessary, as the wadding may become flattened and the padded effect will be lost.

Tack round the quilting along the transferred outline and cut off the surplus close to the stitching. Bind the raw edge with yellow bias binding following the instructions given on page 73.

EXPERIMENTING

Quilting by machine is much quicker to work than by hand, although, unless you are really proficient at machine stitching, it is suitable only for simple designs. Two types of quilting work well in machine stitching: English quilting, described on page 60, and Italian quilting, also known as cord quilting.

For English quilting, prepare the layers of fabric and wadding as if you were going to quilt by hand. Choose a suitable thread to match the content of the top fabric: for example, use cotton or cotton-covered thread on cotton fabric and synthetic thread on polyester/cotton fabric.

Select a medium stitch tension when using the normal machine foot, so that the tacked layers will pass easily underneath. Alternatively, use a special quilting foot which also has a width guide, so that

straight lines do not have to be marked on the fabric. Keep the design simple: simple curves and straight lines forming stripes, checks or diamonds work best. Work alternate lines of stitching in opposite directions to help prevent the fabric puckering.

Italian quilting is worked in an entirely different manner from English quilting, and it is purely decorative. Here, two layers of fabric (a top and a backing fabric) are used without any wadding. The design is outlined by two rows of stitching to make narrow channels in the fabric. A length of special quilting yarn or thin cotton cord is inserted into the channels to raise the pattern on the surface. Once the quilting is finished, a lining fabric is attached to the back of the whole piece. Choose a loosely-woven fabric like muslin for the backing, and line the finished quilted fabric to match the top.

To work Italian quilting by machine, tack the top and backing fabrics together as for English quilting. Use a twin needle in the machine with the normal foot and outline the design with a double row of straight stitches. Alternatively, use an ordinary needle and stitch twice round each shape. Simple designs are most successful – geometric shapes, flowing lines and gentle curves. When you have finished outlining the design, remove the tacking stitches and turn the quilting over.

Thread a large tapestry needle with quilting yarn or cotton cord and insert it along the channels formed by the stitching (diagram 2). Where there is an angle, intersection or break in the design, bring the thread

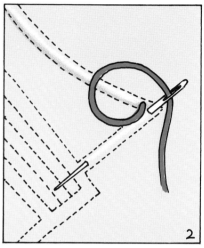

to the surface of the backing fabric and reinsert the needle to leave a small loop on the surface. Cut off the cord at the back (diagram 3).

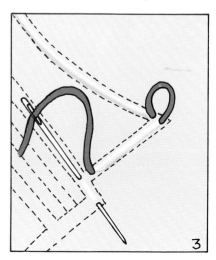

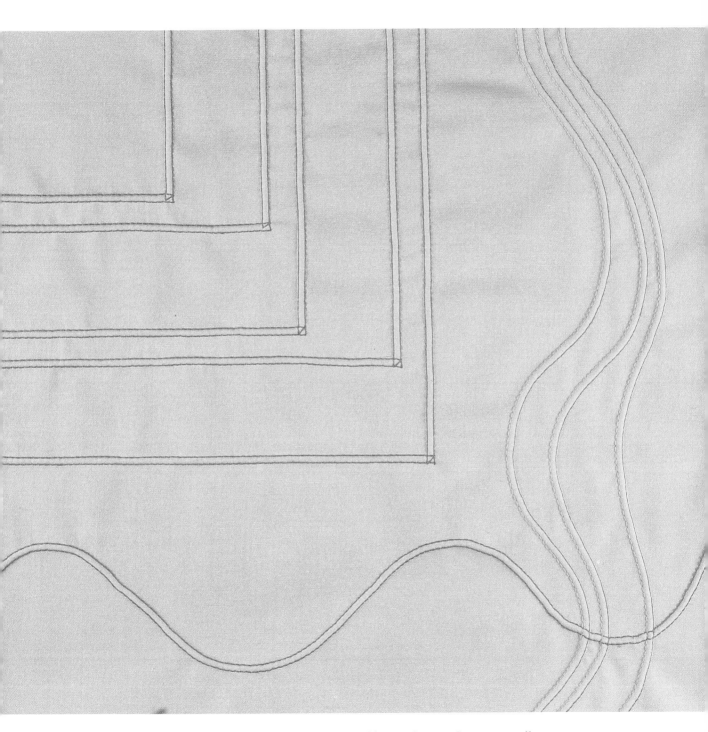

A practice piece of Italian quilting worked by machine with a twin needle

Couching

Couching is used to anchor a thread, group of threads or fine cord to the surface of plain- and even-weave fabrics. This stitch is useful when threads are textured or too thick to pass easily through the fabric. Work on fabric stretched in an embroidery hoop to avoid puckering.

Work couching from right to left. Lay the thread (or threads) on the line to be couched and hold in place with your left hand. Work tiny stitches in a finer thread to hold down the first thread. At the end of the row, pull the ends of both threads through the fabric and secure them on the reverse. Position the couching stitches close together round curves and work one or two extra stitches to turn a corner and retain a good shape.

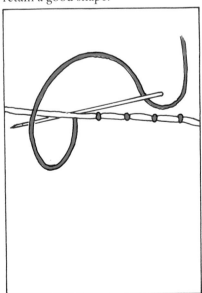

Fly stitch

Fly stitch is used either as a line or filling stitch on both plain- and even-weave fabrics. The Y-shaped stitches are repeated from left to right along a row or used individually to create a filling. Fly stitch is best worked on fabric mounted in an embroidery hoop.

Each stitch is worked separately. Bring the needle through at the left and insert it back into the fabric to the right of this point and diagonally to make a V-shaped loop, as shown. Keep the loop underneath the needle. Pull the needle through and draw up the thread, then work a vertical stitch or 'tail' to secure the loop on the fabric. Work stitches side by side to make a horizontal row, as shown, or place them underneath each other to make a vertical row.

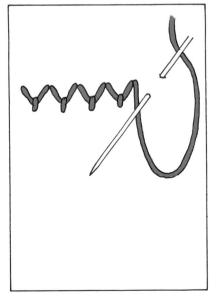

Daisy stitch

(Also known as 'lazy daisy stitch'.) Each daisy stitch is a separate ordinary chain stitch (page 48). This stitch is often worked in groups on plain-weave fabrics to make leaf and flower shapes, but the stitches can be scattered at random to make a filling.

Work daisy stitch in the same way as chain stitch, but secure each loop on the fabric with a small vertical stitch, as shown, before proceeding to make the next chain.

French knot

French knots are used individually to provide dots of colour on both plain- and even-weave fabrics, but they can also be arranged close together to make a textured filling. French knots are a little difficult to work at first and you will need to practise them to get the correct effect. For best results, always work with your fabric mounted in an embroidery hoop.

Bring the thread on to the surface of the fabric and hold it taut with your left hand. Twist the needle round the thread two or three times and tighten the twists. Still holding the thread taut, turn the needle round and insert it into the fabric very close to the point where it originally emerged. To finish the knot, carefully pull the needle and thread through the twists.

Bring the thread through the fabric, and insert the needle a short distance away, allowing the point to emerge at the same place as the thread. Wrap the thread round the needle six or seven times to make a coil. Hold the coil down on the fabric with your left thumb, then pull the needle through. To make the coil lie flat on the surface, pull the thread gently in the opposite direction and insert the needle in the same place as before.

Make a foundation of an even number of spokes. Do this by working eight or twelve straight stitches of identical length radiating from the same point. Alternatively, for an eight-spoke web, work an ordinary cross stitch (page 56) over an upright cross made from two straight stitches.

Using a tapestry needle, work back stitches (page 48) over the spokes, as shown, without picking up the ground fabric. Start at the centre and work outwards in a spiral. Take the thread through to the back of the fabric to finish.

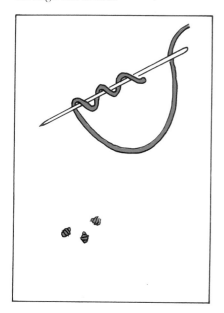

Bullion knot

Bullion knots are used in the same way as French knots, but this stitch produces long coiled knots with a heavier appearance. Bullion knots also need practice and should be worked on fabric mounted in an embroidery hoop. Use a thick needle with a small eye to pass through the coil of thread without difficulty.

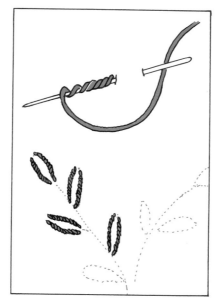

Ribbed spider's web

Ribbed spider's web makes a strong circular shape with raised spokes radiating from the centre of a circle. Use spider's webs in different sizes on both plain- and even-weave fabrics when you need a spot of solid colour. It can also be worked in two contrasting colours.

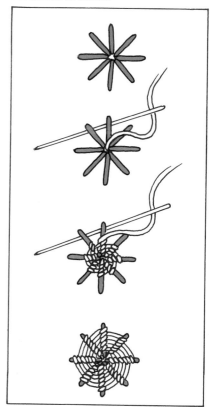

FESTIVE TABLECLOTH

Just the thing for a special Christmas gathering, this overcloth is
made from snowy white fabric, hand-painted with festive motifs
in bright colours.

Featuring hand-painting and simple
embroidery stitches, the finished effect looks
complicated but it is surprisingly
straightforward to make. The motifs are first
coloured with special fabric paints which are
made colourfast by ironing on the reverse,
then outlined with back stitch to give each
motif a crisp, well-defined edge.

Keep the overcloth quite short, so that the
bound edge sits neatly in your lap when sitting
down, and lay it over a floor-length, bright
green undercloth made in the same way.
Enhance the effect by making a set of matching
napkins to complete the setting, decorating
each one with a scaled-down motif in one
corner.

REQUIREMENTS

Medium weight white and
  green cotton or polyester/
  cotton fabric, see next
  page for quantity
Fabric paint in the following
  colours: scarlet, green,
  gold
Stranded cotton in the
  following colours: scarlet,
  green, yellow
Crewel needle size 7

Tacking thread
White, scarlet and green
  sewing thread
25 mm (1 in) wide scarlet
  and green bias binding
Sewing needle and pins
Large embroidery hoop
Small and medium-sized
  artist's soft paintbrushes
Tracing paper
HB pencil

Thin card
Craft knife
Old newspapers
Masking tape
Dressmaker's pattern paper
Drawing pin

MEASURING UP

First measure the diameter of the table top, then sit at the table and measure from the table top down to your lap. For the long undercloth, measure to the floor. Double the length in each case and add to the diameter of the table. You need not add a hem allowance for bound edges.

When the diameter of the cloth is less than the width of your chosen fabric, then one length of fabric will be sufficient. When the diameter exceeds the fabric width, for example when making the floor-length cloth, you will need to join two or more fabric widths together, unless you have chosen extra wide sheeting fabric. Join long strips of fabric to both sides of a central panel to avoid an unsightly centre seam.

To do this, cut one piece of fabric to the same length as the diameter of the tablecloth. Cut the remaining fabric in half lengthwise and join one strip to each side of the first length to make a square, matching the selvages to make neat seams underneath the cloth.

Join the strips together with a plain seam (page 81), taking a 1.5 cm (5⁄8 in) seam allowance. Press the seams open.

CUTTING OUT

Fold the square of white fabric in half with right sides facing, then fold in half again to make a square. Mark the corner which is the centre of the fabric with three or four tacking stitches.

Make a paper pattern by cutting a square of paper to the same size as the folded fabric. Take a piece of string. Tie one end of the string round a drawing pin and the other end round a pencil. The distance between the pin and the pencil should equal half the diameter of the tablecloth. Place the pin in the corner A of the square and, holding the pencil at right angles to the paper, draw an arc from B to C (see diagram on page 40). Cut out the paper pattern.

Lay the pattern on top of the folded fabric, making sure that corner A lies exactly over the tacked corner. Pin to the fabric and cut out along the curved line. Remove the tacking stitches and open out the cloth. Repeat the process using the green fabric to cut out the full length undercloth.

PAINTING THE MOTIFS

Trace the actual-size holly, bow and bauble motifs opposite. Transfer the shapes to thin card and cut round each one carefully with a craft knife to make a set of templates. Using the photograph as a guide to position on the table top, lay the templates on the white fabric with equal spaces between the motifs, and draw round the outlines with a sharp HB pencil.

If you are unfamiliar with fabric paints, read through the hints on page 70 before starting. Place the fabric over a thick layer of old newspapers covered with tissue or paper towels to keep the newsprint off the fabric. Tape a section down with masking tape to prevent it slipping and smearing the paint. Working with one colour at a time, outline the shapes with fabric paint using the small brush. Fill in the shapes with the larger brush. Allow to dry, then repeat with the other colours, washing the brushes thoroughly between colour changes.

Work round the cloth in sections, taking care to allow each area of paint to dry out thoroughly before moving the fabric. To fix the paint, press on the wrong side following the manufacturer's instructions.

WORKING THE EMBROIDERY

Mount the fabric in the large embroidery hoop (page 16), moving it as necessary, and outline the painted motifs with back stitch (page 48) using the crewel needle with 3 strands of thread throughout, in the colours indicated in the illustration.

For a heavier effect, pick out the details of the design in 3 strands of black or matching thread, using back stitch to work the lines and blocks of satin stitch (page 56) for the tiny solid shapes.

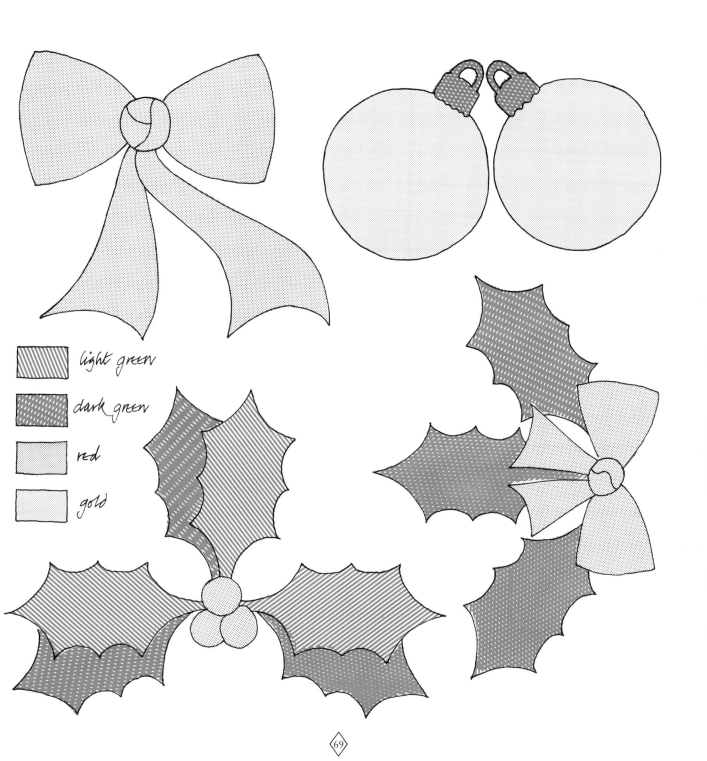

light green

dark green

red

gold

MAKING UP

When all the embroidery has been completed, press the cloth lightly on the wrong side over a well-padded surface with a warm iron.

Finish the edges of both cloths in the same way, by binding them with 25 mm (1 in) wide ready-made bias binding following the instructions on page 73, first method. Bind the painted cloth with scarlet binding and the green cloth with a matching green. Press the hems.

EXPERIMENTING

Combine the flower, heart and bell shapes on this page with the bow from the festive tablecloth on the previous page to create designs with a celebratory theme. Bells and bows decorate a tablecloth for a special wedding anniversary; hearts and flowers provide the theme for a romantic occasion. Choose your colours to reflect the event, silver or gold motifs on white for a wedding anniversary, pink and lavender to make a St Valentine's day setting, yellow and green to celebrate Easter. Put several small motifs together to create an attractive traycloth border, or use the shapes on a large scale for extra impact.

Successful fabric painting

Match fabric and paint carefully. Some paints are suitable only for pure cotton or silk, while other brands can be used on polyester/cotton fabric.

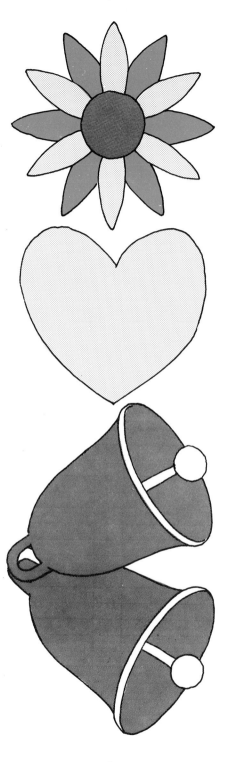

Work on a flat surface protected by layers of newspaper, taping the fabric down with masking tape to prevent it moving and smearing the paint. Keep a box of tissues handy to mop up spills.

Use paints straight from the container after shaking well or stirring thoroughly.

Work in sections, allowing each colour to dry thoroughly before applying the next. Wash out your brushes thoroughly when changing from one colour to another.

Fabric paints can be intermixed to give a wide range of colours. Mixing opaque white with bright colours will give you a range of soft pastels with excellent covering power, but avoid diluting with water as the paint will become thin and difficult to handle.

Fix the design before making up the article, following the individual manufacturer's instructions carefully.

Different colours and different combinations of motifs as a theme for a wedding celebration

Finishing a straight edge

Uneven width hem – Use this hem on medium- and heavyweight fabrics. Fold over the total amount allowed for the hem to the wrong side and press in position. Fold over 6 mm (¼ in) of the raw edge and press. Pin and secure by hand with hemming stitch (below) or by machine stitching (diagram 1).

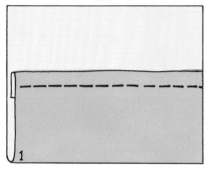

Double hem – Make a double hem on fine and sheer fabrics and also where you need a firm edge. Fold over half the total hem allowance and press in position, then fold over the same amount again and press. Pin in position and secure with hemming stitch (below) or with a row of machine stitching. On slippery fabrics, you may need to tack the hem in place before stitching (diagram 2).

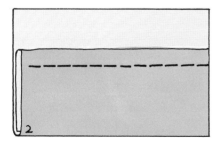

Mitring corners

Mitre corners to reduce bulk and give a neat finish.

Uneven width hem – Fold the hem and press. Unfold the hem once, then draw a diagonal line on the wrong side at the point of the hemline, as shown. Cut off the corner 6 mm (¼ in) outside this line.

Fold back the corner with right sides together, matching the cut edges and the folded edges (diagram 3). Pin and stitch along the marked diagonal line. Turn the corner right side out, press and finish the hem by hand or machine. Slipstitch (see next page) the edges of the mitre together.

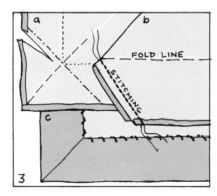

Double hem – Fold the hem and press. Unfold the hem once, then press the corner over as shown so the diagonal fold falls exactly across the corner of the hemline crease. Cut off the corner leaving a 6 mm (¼ in) allowance.

Carefully fold over one side along the hemline crease, press and pin in position. Fold over the other side in the same way. Stitch the hem, either by hand or machine, then slipstitch (below) the edges of the mitre together (diagram 4).

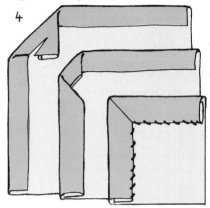

Finishing a circular edge

Make a narrow hem or bind the raw edge using the flat finish method described below. Avoid turning a deeper hem, as the fabric will pull and pucker.

Machine stitch all round 1.5 cm (⅝ in) from the raw edge. Fold over along the stitched line and press so the stitching is just on the wrong side. Fold over 6 mm (¼ in) of the raw edge and press, pin and tack in position. Stitch (diagram 5), remove tacking thread and press, taking care not to stretch the edge.

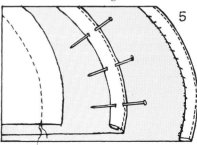

Binding edges

Use the first method when you want the binding to make a decorative feature on the right side, and the second when you would prefer it not to be seen.

Applying bias binding – With the right side of the fabric facing, open out the binding and place the raw edge level with the raw edge of the fabric. Machine stitch along the fold line. Fold binding in half over on to the wrong side of the fabric, enclosing the raw edge. Pin in place and hem by hand along the stitched line (diagram 6).

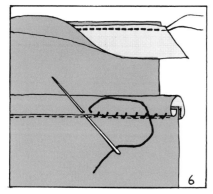

Flat finish binding – Stitch the binding to the right side of the fabric as above, then fold it completely over to the wrong side, taking it past the line of machine stitching, as shown. Pin and hand stitch in place (diagram 7).

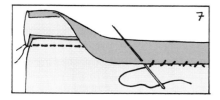

Cutting bias strips

Ready-made bias binding is available in various widths and a wide range of plain colours, but you may prefer to cut your own from patterned fabric.

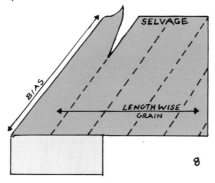

To find the bias of the fabric, lay it flat and fold over one corner at an angle of 45° to the selvage. Mark the fold line with a ruler and dressmaker's pencil, then draw a series of lines parallel to the fold line, having decided on the finished width of the binding, and adding 6 mm (¼ in) to each edge for folding to the wrong side. Cut out with sharp scissors (diagram 8).

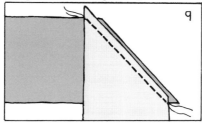

Join the strips together by placing two strips at right angles with right sides facing (diagram 9), pin and stitch them together with a 6 mm (¼ in) seam. Press the seam open

and trim off the surplus triangular shapes. Fold 6 mm (¼ in) to the wrong side down each long edge and press. To finish, fold the binding in half lengthwise and press.

Hemming stitch

Secure the thread inside the hem by working a few small stitches. Take tiny slanting stitches through both the fabric and hem in one movement, as shown. Pick up one or two fabric threads with each stitch and space the stitches evenly along the hem (diagram 10).

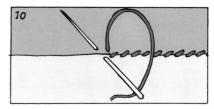

Slipstitch

Secure the thread inside a fold and bring the needle out. Slip the needle along inside the fold of one edge, take the needle across to the other edge and slip along that fold. Gently pull the thread to bring the edges together and repeat (diagram 11).

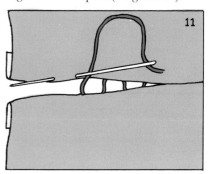

Flowers & Bows
Tablecloth

Swags and bows of turquoise ribbon
combine with bunches of delicate, pastel-coloured flowers
to decorate an attractive small tablecloth.

This design is quick and simple to stitch using satin stitch and French knots and its charm comes from the delightful combination of ribbon and flower colours. To coordinate your table setting, make a set of napkins from matching fabric and embroider one of the tiny flower sprigs in one corner.

This is the type of design which breaks down into several sections and can be adapted easily for other uses. Work the bunches of flowers on their own to decorate the ends of a lace-edged traycloth, or arrange them close together in a ring to make a garland at the centre of a large tablecloth. The ribbon swags and bows can be joined up to make a complete border leaving out the large flower bunches but adding tiny flower sprigs in contrasting thread colours at regular intervals.

Requirements

White firmly-woven cotton or
 linen fabric, see next page
 for amount
Stranded cotton in the
 following colours:
 turquoise, shaded pink,
 lemon, yellow, orange,
 mauve, deep red, white,
 light green, grass green,
 deep green

Crewel needles size 6 and 7
Tacking thread
White sewing thread
Sewing needle and pins
Large embroidery hoop
Tracing paper

METHOD

MEASURING UP

The embroidery was designed to fit a small afternoon tea cloth 108 cm (42 in) square. If you would prefer to make a larger cloth to fit a rectangular table, for example, first measure the length and width of the table top, then decide how far the cloth will hang down over the edge of the table and add twice this measurement to each of the table top measurements. Finally, add 5 cm (2 in) to each measurement for the hem allowance. Remember that fabric is available in several different widths, depending on which type you choose. The fabric width will limit the size of the cloth as this design cannot be successfully worked on fabric which has been joined.

When working the embroidery, extend or shorten the length of the border to suit the dimensions of your cloth by working more or fewer ribbon swags and bunches of flowers along each side.

WORKING THE EMBROIDERY

Trace and enlarge the design elements (opposite) to the size required. Cut out the fabric. Using the photograph as a guide to position, transfer the swags, floral motifs and corner sections to the fabric by one of the methods shown on page 24.

Mount the fabric in the embroidery hoop, moving it as necessary when the motifs have been stitched.

Embroider the swags and bows in satin stitch (page 56) using the size 6 crewel needle and six strands of turquoise thread.

Work the flowers in satin stitch, star stitch (see below) and French knots (page 64). Work the leaves and stems in stem stitch (page 48), following the colours shown on the photograph. Use the size 7 crewel needle and three strands of thread for the leaves and small flowers, and six strands in the size 6 needle for the remaining flowers.

Star stitch

Star stitch is easy to work. It consists of evenly-spaced straight stitches arranged to form a circle.

Work six or eight straight stitches of identical length radiating from the centre of the circle (diagram 1).

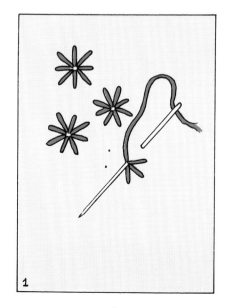

1

MAKING UP

When all the embroidery has been completed, press lightly on the wrong side over a well-padded surface. Use a warm iron and take care not to press too hard, which would crush the stitching.

Turn up a double hem (page 72) round the cloth and mitre the corners (page 72). Make sure that the embroidered border is an equal distance from the hem edge at each side. Hand sew the hem with matching thread and hemming stitch (page 73). Press the hem.

EXPERIMENTING

The outline flowers on the next page can be worked in a variety of ways to decorate tablecloths, napkins, tablemats and traycloths. Embroider them in the same way as the flowers on this page or adapt several for use with some of the other techniques shown in this book. For example, the poppy motif would look equally effective embroidered with a shaded thread using long and short stitch (page 56), outlined in back stitch (page 48) and coloured in with fabric paint (page 70), or repeated to make a design for hand quilting (page 60).

Enlarge the flower shapes (page 78), cut them out of medium weight cotton fabric and apply to a background fabric with blanket stitch as shown on page 49. Mix plain and patterned fabrics to make the flowers, or cut the shapes out of

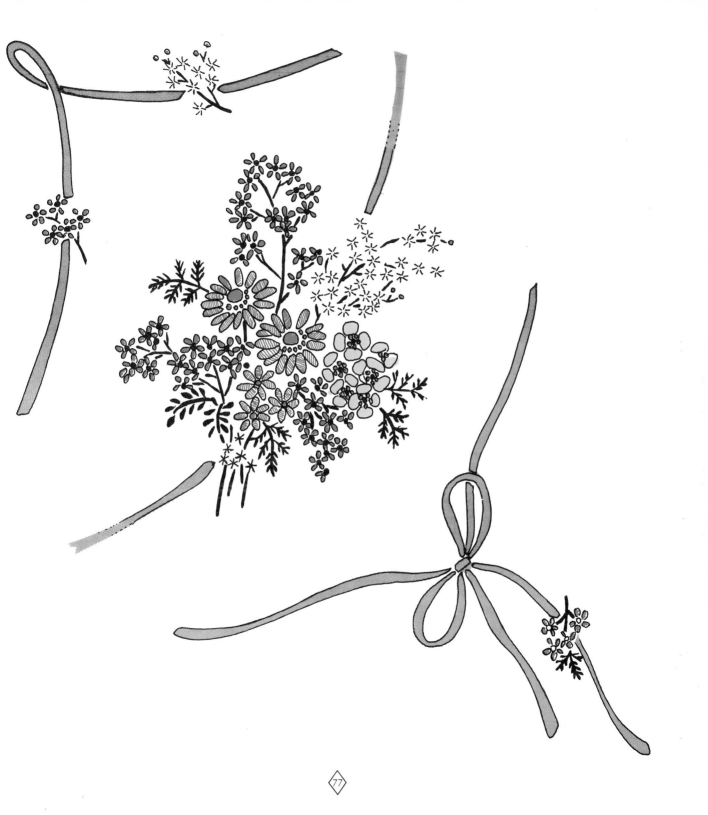

plain fabric and apply them to a background printed with a tiny all-over pattern. You could trace off the heart and bell motifs given on page 70 and apply these in the same way, perhaps adding surface embroidery in the form of French knots and bullion knots (pages 64 and 65) for extra decoration.

Simple shapes, such as the tulip and daisy motifs, translate easily into a chart for cross stitch embroidery. To do this, you will first need to buy ready-graphed tracing paper or make your own by ruling a small-scale grid on to ordinary tracing paper with a fine-point waterproof marker.

Lay the paper over the motif and trace the outline, adjusting the shapes to fit the grid squares. Use a pencil at this stage as you may need to make several alterations to achieve a pleasing result. When you are finally satisfied with the design, draw over the pencil lines with the waterproof marker. This will make a squared outline design which you can then transfer square by square on to ordinary graph paper. Fill in the various sections with coloured pencils or felt-tipped pens to indicate the different thread colours needed.

By repeating several motifs in a row, you will have a border pattern which can be worked in cross stitch (page 56) on a piece of even-weave fabric. When making a continuous border round all sides of a square of fabric, work out the corner design by following the suggestions given on page 54.

Try making a cross stitch chart of the swags, bows and flowers on the previous page, remembering that you will probably need to enlarge the design considerably in order to make the shapes large enough to work with comfortably. Other designs with motifs which can be translated into charts, are the festive tablecloth (page 66) and the abstract place setting on page 26.

Tulips translated into a cross stitch design from the motif opposite

Scalloped edge

A scalloped edge can be worked on both rectangular and circular tablecloths.

For a rectangular cloth, trace and enlarge one of the scallop shapes (diagram 1) to the desired size. Use the tracing to cut a template from thin card. Place the template on the wrong side of the fabric and draw round the edge with a dressmaker's pencil. Repeat along the edge of the fabric.

To mark scallops round a circular edge, make a paper pattern to the same size and shape as the finished cloth. Divide the edge into small equal sections and mark a scallop in each one by drawing round a drinking glass of similar diameter. Transfer the scallops to the fabric using one of the transfer methods given on page 24, or cut out the pattern and carefully draw round each scallop.

Embroider in buttonhole stitch (page 49) or machine satin stitch, then cut away the surplus fabric close to the edge (diagram 2). You can vary the depth of the embroidery so it is deepest at the bottom of each scallop and quite narrow where they join together. To do this mark both an inside and outside edge on the fabric.

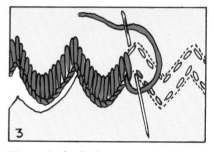

Chevron edge

Use this edging on rectangular cloths and napkins.

Make a paper pattern to the same size and shape as the finished item. Divide the edge into sections and

mark a triangle of identical size in each one. The depth of the border can be adjusted by making shallow or deep triangles. Transfer the chevrons to the fabric as described for the circular cloth above. Embroider in buttonhole stitch (page 49) or use narrow machine satin stitch. Cut away the surplus fabric close to the edge (diagram 3).

Hem stitched edge

Finish rectangular cloths, mats and napkins made from even-weave linen in this way. The embroidery is worked just above the hem as a decoration and also to secure the hem. Hem stitch is easy to work, although you may prefer to use antique hem stitch as the effect on the right side is neater.

Hem stitch – Draw out the required number of threads, turn the hem up so that the fold lies just along the edge of the drawn threads. Tack in place. Working with the right side facing, bring the needle through at the left and pick up three or four vertical threads from right to left, as shown. Insert the needle so it pierces the hem at the back and bring it out at the front just to the right of the threads. Tighten the

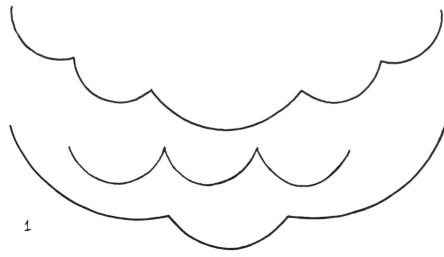

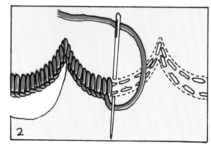

working thread to bunch the fabric threads. Repeat along the row, making sure you pick up the hem with each stitch (diagram 4).

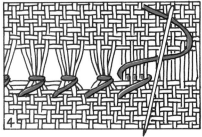

Antique hem stitch – Prepare the hem as for hem stitch, but this time work with the wrong side of the fabric facing. Bring the needle through at the left and pick up three or four vertical threads from right to left, then slip the needle in between the hem, as shown, bringing it out to the right of the group of threads. Tighten the working thread to bunch the fabric threads and repeat along the row (diagram 5). The lower diagram shows the effect on the right side.

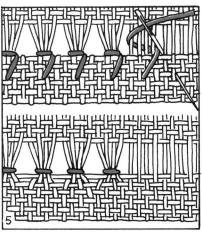

Frilled edge

Single or double frills make a luxurious edging for full-length circular tablecloths. Vary the length of your frill from one and a half to three times the length of the edge to which it will be stitched, depending on the fullness required.

Single frill – Calculate the depth of the frill and add 1.5 cm (⅝ in) for the seam allowance and, depending on the weight of the fabric, between 1 cm and 2 cm (½ in–¾ in) for a double hem.

Join the short edges together with a flat fell seam (below) to make a continuous strip. Make a double hem (page 72) along the lower edge. Divide the frill and the fabric edge into an equal number of sections. Work two rows of large running stitches (page 48) along each frill section and pull up to fit the fabric sections (diagram 6).

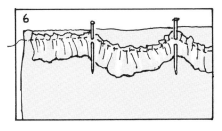

With right sides together, pin the frill to the fabric edge, tack and stitch. Neaten the seam with machine zigzag and press upwards.

Double frill – Cut double the required depth plus twice the top seam allowance. Use a plain seam (below) to stitch the lengths

together and make a continuous strip. Fold in half, matching the raw edges, and gather and attach in the same way as for a single frill.

Plain seam

Place the fabric with right sides together and raw edges level. Pin, tack and stitch 1.5 cm (⅝ in) from raw edge. Press open (diagram 7).

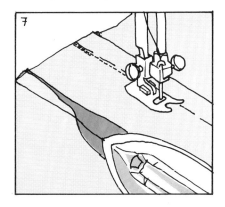

Flat fell seam

Make a plain seam along the raw edge and press both the seam allowances to one side. Trim the underneath allowance to 6 mm (¼ in). Fold the top allowance in half to enclose the trimmed edge, as shown. Press the fold flat, pin and stitch close to the edge (diagram 8).

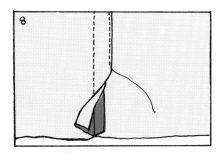

LACE-TRIMMED OVERCLOTH

Make a pretty lace-trimmed overcloth to cover a small round occasional table, displaying it over a long frilled undercloth made out of printed chintz.

Dress up a small occasional table with layers of fabric to create a focal point in your room, at the same time disguising a less-than-perfect piece of furniture. Begin with a floor-length chintz undercloth trimmed with a frilled hem, then add a lavishly decorated square cloth over the top.

For a variety of effects using the same top cloth, make several undercloths from plain or patterned fabric in different colours, perhaps adding a third layer in a contrasting colour between the two cloths for a really luxurious look. The overcloth is decorated with applied lace motifs, beads and hand embroidery.

REQUIREMENTS

Lightweight white cotton fabric, plain or with a woven, self-coloured pattern, see next page for amount
Printed chintz with a white or cream background, see next page for amount
White cotton lace with a pattern of large motifs e.g. flowers, birds

White cotton lace edging 1.5 cm (5⁄8 in) deep and long enough to edge the cloth
Stranded cotton in the following colours: white, cream
Soft embroidery cotton in the following colours: white, cream, pale grey
Small crystal and pearl beads

Narrow double satin ribbon in cream and white
Crewel needle size 7
Chenille needle size 20
Beading needle
Tacking thread
White sewing thread
Sewing needle and pins
Large embroidery hoop

MEASURING UP FOR THE OVERCLOTH

Measure across the table top and add between 15 and 25 cm (6 and 10 in) for the overhang at each side, depending on the height of your table. Finally, add 1.5 cm (⅝ in) all round for the hem allowance.

MEASURING UP FOR THE UNDERCLOTH

Measure the diameter of the table top, then measure right down to the floor. Multiply the second measurement by two and add to the diameter. If you wish to add a frill round the edge, subtract twice the depth of the finished frill from the overall measurement. For a cloth without a frill, add 1.5 cm (⅝ in) all round for the hem allowance. Should you need to join lengths of fabric to make this cloth, use the method given on page 40, and match the pattern as described below. You may need to buy extra fabric if you are matching a large pattern.

JOINING PATTERNED FABRICS

Tack fabric pieces together in this way before stitching and the pattern will match perfectly.

Press the seam allowance to the wrong side on one of the edges. Overlap this edge over the other, so that the raw edges are level and the pattern matches. Pin in place (diagram 1).

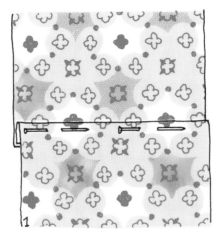

Working from the right side of the fabric, and using tacking thread, take the needle along the folded edge for about 1.5 cm (⅝ in), take it across to the flat fabric and take a stitch of identical size along the seamline (diagram 2).

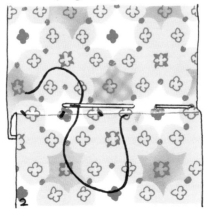

Continue along the fold in the same way so that the two pieces are joined by a row of tiny horizontal stitches. Finally, fold the pieces with right sides together and join with a flat fell seam (page 81). Remove the tacking stitches.

WORKING THE EMBROIDERY

Cut out the white fabric to the required size. Cut out four separate motifs from the lace and tack them in position at each corner of the fabric.

Mount the fabric in the large embroidery hoop (page 16), moving it as necessary. Using running stitch (page 48) and 3 strands of white thread in the crewel needle, stitch round portions of the lace motifs to define the shapes and also anchor the lace to the fabric. Outline the motif with large back stitches (page 48) worked in 3 strands of white thread (diagram 3).

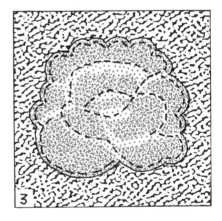

Make tiny bows from the ribbon, then stitch them on to the lace motifs with 3 strands of matching thread. Using white soft cotton couched down with 3 strands of white thread, work two or three flowing rows of couching (page 64) from each bow, taking the stitching across the lace and on to the white fabric, as indicated in diagram 4.

Using white, cream and grey soft cotton and the chenille needle, embroider small groups of French knots and daisy stitches (page 64) close to the bows, as indicated on the diagram.

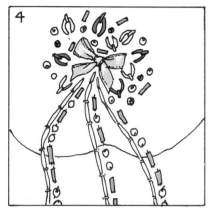

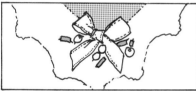

Apply the beads with tiny back stitches, using the beading needle and white sewing thread. Group them near the bows and apply them at intervals along the couched lines (diagram 5).

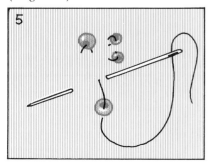

MAKING UP THE OVERCLOTH

When all the embroidery has been completed, remove any visible tacking stitches, then press the cloth very carefully on the wrong side over a well-padded surface using a warm iron, taking care not to press the beaded areas.

Turn up a narrow double hem (page 72) round the cloth and fold the corners neatly. Pin, tack and machine stitch the hem using matching thread.

Pin the lace edging round the cloth, positioning it over the hem on the right side to hide the row of machine stitching. Make several tiny pleats at each corner so the lace lays flat. Tack in place, then stitch down with a row of back stitch in 3 strands of white thread.

To complete the cloth, decorate the lace edging at intervals with ribbon bows and tiny groups of crystal and pearl beads.

MAKING UP THE UNDERCLOTH

Cut out and make up the undercloth as described on page 68. To make and apply the frill, follow the instructions given on page 81.

EXPERIMENTING

Coverings for occasional tables need not be laundered frequently, unlike other articles of table linen which come in contact with food and drink. This means you can use a less practical fabric, such as satin, velvet or pure silk as a background for the embroidered decoration, perhaps picking up one of the colours in the printed undercloth, and have the cloth dry cleaned.

Cotton lace is usually only available in white or cream, but you can easily dye it at home. Dye the lace in one piece, as separate motifs fray badly. Use a suitable dye for natural fibres and always follow the manufacturer's instructions for dyeing and fixing the colour. The dyes are usually available in liquid or powder form, and colours can often be intermixed to give a more subtle colour range.

Instead of using lace, experiment with cut-out net shapes. Dress net made from synthetic fibres is inexpensive and comes in a range of both bright and pastel colours. Net can look very effective when applied in the same way as lace, but try to keep the shapes large and simple in outline. By overlapping one shape on another you can achieve interesting colour variations. Edge the cloth with a narrow net frill or apply net rosettes around the hem.

When working with net, remember that its regular structure can be used as a grid for keeping counted thread stitches even in the same way as even-weave fabric (page 36). Both cross stitch (page 56) and the three variations of herringbone stitch described on page 57 can be worked on net with good results.

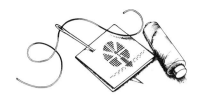

FLORAL TABLECLOTH

Designed for the needlewoman who loves flowers, this
delightful tablecloth features different floral motifs
worked in a riotous paintbox of colours.

Floral designs are always popular among stitchers and craftspeople as they have an almost timeless quality. Tablelinen decorated with flowers adds freshness and charm to any table setting, whether formal or informal, and shows off delicately-patterned china to full advantage.

Each motif is positioned on its own square of fabric, separated by crossing rows of threaded stem stitch. The design allows you plenty of scope to show off your technical abilities as many of the areas of solid embroidery are cleverly shaded in long and short stitch using several colours of thread. For the less experienced stitcher, choose a selection of ready-shaded threads and work a single floral motif in each corner of a smaller square of fabric to use as an overcloth.

MEASURING UP

The tablecloth shown in the photograph measures 108 cm (42 in) square and it is divided by rows of threaded stem stitch into sixteen 27 cm (10½ in) squares each containing a floral motif. The design would be equally successful worked on a larger scale, to decorate either a square or rectangular tablecloth, providing the fabric joins are positioned where they can be disguised beneath the rows of threaded stem stitch.

Keeping this in mind, should you wish to make a larger tablecloth than the one described, measure up in the following way. First measure the length and width of the table top; decide how far the cloth will hang down over the edge of the table and add twice this measurement to each of the table top measurements. You will need to adjust these figures until they are multiples of 27 cm (10½ in). Alternatively, you could make each square slightly larger or smaller if this would be more convenient for the size of your table. Finally, add 5 cm (2 in) to each measurement for the hem allowance.

PREPARING THE FABRIC

To prepare the fabric for the embroidery, you must first tack the position of the crossing lines.

Cut out the fabric to the required size and make any necessary joins (see above). Turn up the hem allowance and tack temporarily in position. Next, divide one edge of the cloth into 27 cm (10½ in) sections and mark each section with a pin. Repeat on opposite side.

Beginning at one side, fold the fabric between the first pair of pins and press the fold very lightly. Tack along the fold. Working across the cloth, repeat for each section, then press flat. Repeat this procedure in the opposite direction to divide the cloth into identically-sized squares.

WORKING THE EMBROIDERY

Trace and enlarge the motifs (page 89) to the size indicated on the diagrams. Transfer one motif to the centre of each square using one of the methods described on page 24 or 25.

Mount the fabric in the embroidery hoop, moving it as necessary when the motifs have been worked. Embroider the motifs using the size 7 crewel needle and three strands of thread throughout. Work the petals and leaves in long and short stitch, satin stitch (page 56) and buttonhole stitch (page 49), and the details in stem stitch (page 48) and French knots (page 64), using the photograph as a guide and blending the shaded areas carefully.

MAKING UP

When all the flower motifs have been completed, press lightly on the wrong side over a well-padded surface. Use a warm iron and take care not to press too hard, which would crush the stitching.

Remove the temporary tacking round the hem and make a narrow double hem (page 72), turning in the corners neatly. Hem by hand or machine and press the hem lightly.

Using six strands of light beige thread in the size 6 crewel needle, work rows of stem stitch along the tacked lines, taking the stitches right across the hem and securing the thread ends neatly on the wrong side. Work all the rows in one direction first, then cross them with lines worked in the opposite direction. Remove all the tacking.

Using the tapestry needle threaded with six strands of dark beige thread, lace this thread up and down behind the stem stitches, as shown in diagram 1, without picking up any ground fabric. Give the cloth a final light press as described above.

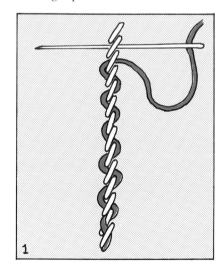

1

110 MM (4'4")

110 MM (4'4")

110 MM (4'4")

160 MM (6'4")

EXPERIMENTING

The selection of floral motifs given here and on the previous page can be used to decorate table linen in a variety of ways. Simple adaptations of the tablecloth on page 86 can be very attractive: you could omit the threaded stem stitch lines, for example, but as this is a formal arrangement you would still need to divide the fabric into squares with tacking stitches to position the motifs accurately. Alternatively,

arrange the motifs informally by scattering them round the edge of the cloth. You may choose to keep the dividing lines, but repeat just one or two of the motifs, arranging them on alternate squares to give a chequerboard effect.

Substituting other line stitches for the threaded stem stitch will also change the effect. Back stitch or running stitch (page 48) would give a fine, delicate line and both these stitches can be threaded with a

second colour in a similar manner to stem stitch; while a row of chain stitch (page 48) would be much heavier. Couching (page 64) can be used to attach fine cord, narrow ribbon or a metallic thread, but check on their after-care requirements as dry-cleaning may be necessary for some of these.

You can create a different appearance by using several threads and weights of thread to work the floral motifs. A bold, rather solid effect is created by six strands of stranded cotton for example, or perlé cotton can be used to make the stitching stand out well from the background fabric. If you chose to work with soft cotton, you would need to enlarge the motifs and work on a fabric with a more open weave, as this is much heavier than perlé or stranded cotton, but the soft, matt appearance of the stitching is attractive.

For a luxurious finish, highlight some of the small details of the flowers by working French knots in a pure silk stranded thread. Silk thread, although rather expensive and impractical for working large areas of embroidery on tablelinen, looks very attractive when mixed in tiny amounts with cotton threads. When shading, try mixing one strand of silk with two or three of stranded cotton in toning colours and using these through the needle together. The fabric will need to be dry-cleaned as silk thread is not always colour-fast.

CARE AND CONSERVATION

Avoid placing any embroidered article in direct sunlight or near a heat source, as both light and heat cause colours to fade and the fibres of fabrics and threads to weaken and become brittle.

Always take immediate first aid measures to limit the damage as soon as a stain occurs. Mop up spilled liquids, such as fruit juice and red wine, with tissues or paper towels and rinse the affected portion under tepid running water. Scrape off spilled foods, then blot the fabric with tissues before washing in the normal way as quickly as possible.

Persistent stains should be treated with the appropriate solvent or a brand-name stain remover, first testing its suitability on an inconspicuous area of fabric. Alternatively, seek specialist advice. Repeat mild treatments several times in preference to using a harsh, heavy-duty solvent.

Similarly, repair tears, darn worn areas and patch holes as soon as possible to prevent the damage to the fabric getting any worse. Small pieces of matching fabric are useful for patching and for removing fabric threads to work a darn. Keep oddments of embroidery threads, too, as in some cases, you may be able to embroider an extra motif to disguise a repair.

When laundering embroidered table linen, wash carefully by hand in hand-hot water with a mild, detergent-free cleaning agent. Dry out of direct sunlight. Gently ease the article into shape while damp and press on the wrong side before the fabric dries out completely.

You can use old-fashioned laundry starch to achieve a crisp finish on formal table linen. Always press embroidered articles face down over a well-padded surface, taking great care not to crush the stitching. If you are at all worried that an article may not be completely colourfast, then have it dry-cleaned by a specialist firm.

To look after your table linen when not in use, always make sure it is perfectly clean and dry before storing. Avoid the use of polythene bags which attract dirt and dust and also prevent natural fibres like linen and cotton from breathing. Instead, loosely fold the article between protective layers of white, acid-free tissue paper, making sure that each fold is padded with tissue. Store in a clean fabric cover, in a dark, dry and moth-free place. For long-term storage, roll each one right-side out round a cardboard tube, protecting each layer with acid-free tissue and store in a fabric cover as before.

GLOSSARY

Aida A type of *even-weave* fabric.

Bias binding A strip cut diagonally across the warp and weft threads of a piece of fabric.

Binca *Even-weave* fabric similar to *Aida* but with a coarser weave.

Bonding web/Transfer fusing web An iron-on fabric used to sandwich two pieces of fabric together permanently.

Card/Cardboard or Lightweight illustration board Used for *templates.*

Coton à broder/Brilliant embroidery cotton A highly-twisted, fine cotton embroidery thread.

Drawing pin/Thumb tack Used to anchor string when cutting a circular pattern.

Even-weave fabric Fabric woven with warp and weft threads of identical thickness providing the same number of threads over a given area.

Dressmaker's pattern paper/Large graph paper Paper marked out with a regular grid useful for pattern cutting.

Ground fabric The background fabric on which embroidery is worked.

Perlé cotton/Pearl cotton A twisted embroidery thread with a lustrous sheen.

Perspex/Clear plastic Useful substitute for glass when making a light box.

Plain-weave/Common weave fabric Fabric in which the weft threads weave alternately under and over the warp.

Pounce powder A special powder for marking out a design directly onto the *ground fabric*. Talcum powder for dark fabrics can also be used, with a little charcoal added for light fabrics.

Soft embroidery cotton/Matte embroidery cotton A thick, matt-finish embroidery thread.

Stranded cotton/Embroidery floss A loosely-twisted, six strand embroidery thread which can be separated for fine work.

Tack, tacking/Baste, basting A large, temporary running stitch.

Template A piece of *card* cut to the shape of a portion of a design – used for transferring designs.

Wadding/Batting Padding fabric made from cotton or synthetic fibres.

ACKNOWLEDGEMENTS

With thanks to the following companies for supplying props for the photography:

David Mellor, 4 Sloane Square, London SW1 (cutlery)

Coats Leisure Crafts Group Ltd, 39 Durham Street, Glasgow G41 1BS (embroidery threads and fabrics)

INDEX